CONTENTS

List of Illustrations .... *(follows contents)*
Preface to the First Edition 5
Preface to the Second Edition 8
Preface to the American Edition .... *(follows page 18)*
Introduction *19*
Le Mystère des Cathédrales 33
Paris 67
Amiens 121
Bourges 137
The Cyclic Cross of Hendaye 163
Conclusion 173
Index *179*

LIST OF ILLUSTRATIONS

The Sphinx protects and controls Science *(Frontispiece)*

I   Our Lady-of-Confession. Black Virgin of the Crypts of St. Victor, Marseilles *(facing page 58)*.

II   Alchemy. Bas-relief on the Great Porch of Notre-Dame, Paris *(facing page 70)*.

III   Notre-Dame, Paris. The Alchemist *(facing page 72)*.

IV   Notre-Dame, Paris. The mysterious Fountain at the foot of the Old Oak *(facing page 74)*.

V   Notre-Dame, Paris — Porch of Judgement. The Alchemist protects the Athenor against external influences *(facing page 78)*.

VI   Notre-Dame, Paris — Central Porch. The Crow-Putrefaction *(facing page 79)*.

VII   Notre-Dame, Paris — Central Porch. Philosophic Mercury *(facing page 82)*.

VIII   Notre-Dame, Paris — Central Porch. The Salamander-Calcination *(facing page 83)*.

IX   Notre-Dame, Paris — Central Porch. Preparation of the Universal Solvent *(facing page 84)*.

X   Notre-Dame, Paris — Central Porch. Evolution — colours and processes of the Great Work *(facing page 85)*.

XI   Notre-Dame, Paris — Central Porch. The four Elements and the two Natures *(facing page 88)*.

XII   Notre-Dame, Paris — Central Porch. The Athenor and the Stone *(facing page 89)*.

XIII   Notre-Dame, Paris — Central Porch. Conjunction of Sulphur and Mercury *(facing page 90)*.

XIV   Notre-Dame, Paris — Central Porch. The Materials necessary for making the Solvent *(facing page 92)*.

XV   Notre-Dame, Paris — Central Porch. The fixed Body *(facing page 94)*.

XVI   Notre-Dame, Paris — Central Porch. Union of the Fixed and the Volatile *(facing page 95)*.

XVII   Notre-Dame, Paris — Central Porch. Philosophic Sulphur *(facing page 96)*.

XVIII   Notre-Dame, Paris — Central Porch. Cohabitation *(obverse of plate XVII)*.

XIX   Notre-Dame, Paris — Central Porch. Origin and Result of the Stone *(facing plate XVIII)*.

XX   Notre-Dame, Paris — Central Porch. The Knowledge of Weights *(facing page 97)*.

XXI   Notre-Dame, Paris — Central Porch. The Queen kicks down Mercury, Servus Fugitvus *(facing page 98)*.

XXII   Notre-Dame, Paris — Central Porch. The Reign of Saturn *(facing page 99)*.

XXIII   Notre-Dame, Paris — Central Porch. The Subject of the Wise *(facing page 100)*.

XXIV   Notre-Dame, Paris — Central Porch. The Entrance to the Sanctuary *(facing page 101)*.

XXV   Notre-Dame, Paris — Central Porch. Dissolution. Combat of the two Natures *(facing page 102)*.

XXVI   Notre-Dame, Paris — Portal of the Virgin. The Planetary Metals *(facing page 104)*.

XXVII   Notre-Dame, Paris — Portal of the Virgin. The Dog and the Doves *(facing page 105)*.

Fulcanelli: Master Alchemist

THE SPHINX PROTECTS AND CONTROLS SCIENCE

FULCANELLI:
Master Alchemist

Le Mystère des Cathédrales

Esoteric Interpretation of the Hermetic Symbols of The Great Work

A Hermetic Study of Cathedral Construction

Translated from the French
by Mary Sworder

with Prefaces by Eugene Canseliet, F.C.H.
Introduction by Walter Lang
Preface to the American Edition
by Roy E. Thompson, Jr.

Brotherhood of Life
Las Vegas, Nevada, USA

FULCANELLI
Le Mystère des Cathédrales
et l'interprétation ésotérique des symboles hermétiques du grand œuvre
Published by Société Nouvelle des Éditions Pauvert
©1964, 1979, Paris, France

First published in English by Neville Spearman Ltd., ©1971, London
Reprinted 1977, Sudbury, Suffolk, England

American edition published by Brotherhood of Life, Inc., © 1984
Reprinted 1986, 1991, 2000, 2003

ISBN 0-914732-14-5

BROTHERHOOD OF LIFE, INC.
P.O. BOX 46306
LAS VEGAS, NV 89114-6306
www.brotherhoodoflife.com

Printed in the United States of America

Contents

List of Illustrations

XXVIII   Notre-Dame, Paris — Portal of the Virgin. 'Solve et Coagula' *(facing page 106)*.

XXIX   Notre-Dame, Paris — Portal of the Virgin. The Bath of the Stars. Condensation of the Universal Spirit *(facing page 107)*.

XXX   Notre-Dame, Paris. (Porch of St. Anne — St. Marcellus Pillar) Philosophic Mercury of the Great Work *(facing page 112)*.

XXXI   Symbolic coat of Arms (XIIIth Century) *(facing page 120)*.

XXXII   Sainte-Chapelle, Paris — Southern Stained Glass windows. The Massacre of the Innocents *(facing page 121)*.

XXXIII   Amiens Cathedral — Porch of the Saviour. The Fire of the Wheel *(facing page 124)*.

XXXIV   Amiens Cathedral — Porch of the Saviour. Philosophic Coction *(facing page 126)*.

XXXV   Amiens Cathedral — Central Porch. The Cock and the Fox *(facing page 127)*.

XXXVI   Amiens Cathedral — Porch of St. Firmin. The first Matters *(facing page 132)*.

XXXVII   Amiens Cathedral — Porch of the Virgin Mother. The Philosophers' Dew *(facing page 133)*.

XXXVIII   Amiens Cathedral — Porch of the Virgin Mother. The Seven-rayed Star *(facing page 136)*.

XXXIX   Jacques Coeur's House — Facade. The Scallop Shell *(facing page 140)*.

XL   Jacques Coeur's House — Treasure Chamber. Tristan and Isolde Group *(facing page 141)*.

XLI   Lallemant Mansion — Bracket. The Vessel of the Great Work *(facing page 144)*.

XLII   Lallemant Mansion. The Legend of St. Christopher *(facing page 145)*.

XLIII   Chapel of the Lallemant Mansion. The Golden Fleece *(facing page 152)*.

XLIV   Chapel of the Lallemant Mansion. Capital of Pillar. Right side *(facing page 156)*.

XLV   Lallemant Mansion — Chapel Ceiling (Detail) *(facing page 158)*.

XLVI   Chapel of the Lallemant Mansion. Enigma of the Credence *(facing page 159)*.

XLVII   Hendaye. (Basses-Pyrenees) Cyclic Cross *(facing page 168)*.

XLVIII   Cyclic Cross of Hendaye. The four Sides of the Pedestal *(facing page 169)*.

XLIX   Arles — Church of St. Trophime. Tympanum of the Porch (XIIth Century) *(facing page 173)*.

PREFACE TO THE FIRST EDITION

For a disciple it is an ungrateful and difficult task to introduce a work written by his own Master. It is, therefore, not my intention to analyse here *Le Mystère des Cathédrales,* nor to underline its high tone and its profound teaching. I most humbly acknowledge my incapacity and prefer to give the reader the task of evaluating it and the Brothers of Heliopolis the pleasure of receiving this synthesis made so superbly by one of themselves. Time and truth will do the rest.

For a long time now the author of this book has not been among us. The man has disappeared and I cannot without sorrow recall the image of this industrious and wise Master, to whom I owe all, while lamenting that he should so soon have departed. His numerous friends, those unknown brothers who hoped to obtain from him the solution to the mysterious *Verbum dimissum* (missing Word), will join with me in lamenting his loss.

Having reached the pinnacle of knowledge, could he refuse to obey the commands of Destiny? No man is a prophet in his own country. Perhaps this old saying gives the occult reason for the convulsion produced in the solitary and studious life of a philosopher by the flash of Revelation. Under the influence of that divine flame, the former man is entirely consumed. Name, family, native land, all the illusions, all the errors, all the vanities fall to dust. And, like the phoenix of the poets, a new personality is reborn from the ashes. That, at least, is how the philosophic Tradition would have it.

My Master knew this. He disappeared when the fatal hour struck, when the Sign was accomplished. Who, then, would dare to set himself above the Law? As for me, in spite of the anguish of a painful but inevitable separation, I would act no differently myself if I were to experience today that joyful event, which forces the Adept to flee from the homage of the world.

Fulcanelli is no more. But we have at least this consolation, that his thought remains, warm and vital, enshrined for ever in these pages.

Thanks to him, the Gothic cathedral has yielded up its secret. And it is not without surprise and emotion that we learn how our ancestors fashioned the *first stone* of its foundations, that dazzling gem, more precious than gold itself, on which Jesus built his Church. All Truth, all Philosophy and all Religion rest on this *unique and sacred Stone*. Many people, inflated with presumption, believe themselves capable of fashioning it; yet how rare are the elect, those who are sufficiently simple, learned and skilful to complete the task!

But that is of little importance. It is enough for us to know that the wonders of the Middle Ages hold the same positive truth, the same scientific basis as the pyramids of Egypt, the temples of Greece, the Roman catacombs and the Byzantine basilicas.

This is the overall theme of Fulcanelli's book.

The hermeticists—those at least who are worthy of the name—will discover other things here. From the clash of ideas, it is said, light bursts forth; they will recognize here that is from the confrontation of the Book and the Building that the Spirit is released and the Letter dies. Fulcanelli has made the first effort on their behalf; it is up to the hermeticists to make the last. The remaining way is short, but it is essential to be able to recognize it and not to travel without knowing where one is going.

Is something further required?

I know, not from having discovered it myself, but because I was assured of it by the author more than ten years ago, that the *key to the major arcanum is given* quite openly in one of the figures, illustrating the present work. And this key consists quite simply in *a colour* revealed to the artisan right from the first work. No Philosopher, to my knowledge, has emphasized the importance of this essential point. In revealing it, I am obeying the last wishes of Fulcanelli and my conscience is clear.

And now may I be permitted, in the name of the Brothers of Heliopolis and in my own name, warmly to thank the artist, to whom my master has entrusted the illustration of his work. For it is indeed due to the sincere and scrupulous talent of the artist Julien Champagne that *Le Mystère des Cathédrales* is able to wrap its esotericism in a superb cloak of original plates.

E. CANSELIET

F.C.H.

October 1925

PREFACE TO THE SECOND EDITION

When *Le Mystère des Cathédrales* was written down in 1922, Fulcanelli had not yet received the *Gift of God*, but he was so close to supreme Illumination that he judged it necessary to wait and to keep the anonymity, which he had always observed—more, perhaps, from natural inclination than from strict regard for the rule of secrecy. We must say, certainly, that this man of another age, with his strange appearance, his old-fashioned manners and his unusual occupations, involuntarily attracted the attention of the idle, the curious and the foolish. ·Much greater, however, was the attention he was to attract a little later by the complete disappearance of his common presence.

Indeed, right from the time that his first writings were compiled, the Master expressed his absolute and unshakeable resolve to keep his real identity in the background and to insist that the label given him by society should be unequivocally exchanged for the pseudonym—already familiar in his case—required by Tradition. This celebrated name is so firmly secured, even to the remotest future, that it would be absolutely impossible for any patronymic, even the most brilliant or most highly esteemed, to be substituted for it.

One should at least realize that the author of a work of such high quality would not abandon it the moment it came into the world, unless he had pertinent and compelling reasons, long pondered, for so doing. These reasons, on a very different plane, led to the renunciation at which we cannot but wonder, since even the loftiest authors are susceptible to the fame that comes from the printed word. It should be said that the case of Fulcanelli is unique in the realm of Letters in our day, since it derives from an infinitely superior code of ethics. In obedience to this, the new Adept attunes his destiny to that of his exalted predecessors, who, like himself, appeared at their appointed time on the great highway like beacons of hope and mercy. What perfect filial duty, carried to the ultimate degree, in order that the eternal, universal and indivisible Truth might continually be reaffirmed in its double aspect, the spiritual and the scientific. Fulcanelli, like most of the Adepts of old, in casting off the worn-out husk of his *former self*, left nothing on the road but the phantom trace of his signature—a signature, whose aristocratic nature is amply shown by his visiting card.

Anyone with knowledge of the alchemical books of the past will accept as a basic premise that oral instruction from master to pupil is the most valuable of all. Fulcanelli received his own initiation in this way, as I myself received mine from him, although I owe it to myself to state that Cyliani had already opened wide for me the great door of the labyrinth during that week in 1915, when the new edition of his little work was published.

In my introduction to the *Douze Clefs de la Philosophie*, I repeated deliberately that Basil Valentine was my Master's *initiator*, partly because this gave me the opportunity to change the epithet;

that is to say to substitute—for the sake of accuracy—*first* initiator for *true* initiator, which I had used before in my Preface to the *Demeures Philosophales*. At that time I did not know of the very moving letter, which I shall quote a little later, which owes its striking effect to the warm enthusiasm and fervent expression of the writer. Both writer and recipient remain anonymous, because the signature has been scratched out and there is no superscription. The recipient was undoubtedly Fulcanelli's master and Fulcanelli left this revealing letter among his own papers. It bears two crossed brown lines at the folds, from having been kept for a long time in his pocket book, which did not, however, protect it from the fine, greasy dust of the enormous stove going all the time. So, for many years, the author of *Le Mystère des Cathédrales* kept as a talisman the written proof of the triumph of his *true initiator*, which nothing any longer prevents me from publishing; especially since it provides us with a powerful and correct idea of the sublime level at which the Great Work takes place. I do not think that anyone will object to the length of this strange epistle, and it would certainly be a pity to shorten it by a single word:

'My old friend,

'This time you have really had the *Gift of God*; it is a great blessing and, for the first time, I understand how rare this favour is. Indeed, I believe that, in its unfathomable depth of simplicity, the arcanum cannot be found by the force of reason alone, however subtle and well trained it may be. At last you possess the *Treasure of Treasures*. Let us give thanks to the Divine Light which made you a participant in it. Moreover, you have richly deserved it on account of your unshakeable belief in Truth, the constancy of your effort, your perseverence in sacrifice and also, let us not forget . . . *your good works*.

'When my wife told me the good news, I was stunned with surprise and joy and was so happy that I could hardly contain myself. So much so, that I said to myself: let us hope that we shall not have to pay for this hour of intoxication with some terrible aftermath. But, although I was only briefly informed about the matter, I believed that I understood it, and what confirms me in my certainty *is that the fire goes out only when the Work is accomplished and the whole tinctorial mass impregnates the glass, which, from decantation to decantation, remains absolutely saturated and becomes luminous like the sun.*

'You have extended generosity to the point of associating us with' this high and occult knowledge, to which you have full right and which is entirely personal to you. We, more than any, can appreciate its worth and we, more than any, are capable of being eternally grateful to you for it. You know that the finest phrases, the most eloquent protestations, are not worth as much as the moving simplicity of this single utterance: *you are good*, and it is for this great virtue that God has crowned you with the diadem of true royalty. He knows that you will make noble use of the sceptre and of the priceless endowment which it provides. We have for a long time known you as the blue mantle of your friends in trouble. This charitable cloak has suddenly grown larger and your noble shoulders are now covered by the whole azure of the sky and its great sun. May you long enjoy this great and rare good fortune, to the joy and consolation of your friends, and even of your enemies, for misfortune cancels out everything. From henceforth you will have at your disposal the magic ring which works all miracles.

'My wife, with the inexplicable intuition of sensitives, had a really strange dream. She saw a man enveloped in all the colours of the rainbow and raised up to the sun. We did not have long to wait for the explanation. What a miracle! What a beautiful and triumphant reply to my letter, so crammed with arguments and—theoretically—so exact; but yet how far from the *Truth*, from *Reality*. Ah! One can almost say that he, who has greeted the *morning star* has for ever lost the use of his sight and his reason, because he is fascinated by this false light and cast into the abyss. . . . Unless, as in your case, a great stroke of fate comes to pull him unexpectedly from the edge of the precipice.

'I am longing to see you, my old friend, to hear you tell me about the last hours of anguish and of triumph. But be assured that I shall never to able to express in words the great joy that we have felt and all the gratitude we have at the bottom of our hearts. Alleluia!
'I send you my love and congratulations'

'Your old. . . .

'He who knows how to do the Work *by the one and only mercury* has found the most perfect thing—that is to say he has received the light and accomplished the Magistery.'

One passage may perhaps have disconcerted the attentive reader, who is already familiar with the main ideas of the hermetic problem. This was when the intimate and wise correspondent exclaimed: 'Ah! One can almost say that he, who has greeted the *morning star* has for ever lost the use of his sight and his reason, because he is fascinated by their false light and cast into the abyss.'

Does not this phrase apparently contradict what I stated twenty years ago, in a study of the *Golden Fleece*,[1] namely that the star is the great sign of the Work; that it sets its seal on the philosophic matter; that it teaches the alchemist that he has found not the light of fools but the light of the wise; that it is the crown of wisdom; and that it is called the *morning star*?

It may have been noted that I specified briefly that the hermetic star is admired first of all in the *mirror of the art* or *mercury*, before being discovered in the *chemical sky*, where it shines in an infinitely more discreet manner. Torn between my charitable duty to the reader and the need for preserving secrecy, I might have made a virtue of paradox, and, pleading arcane wonders, could then have recopied some lines written in a very old exercise book, after one of those learned talks by Fulcanelli. Those talks, accompanied by cold sweet coffee, were the delight of my assiduous and studious adolescence, when I was greedy for priceless knowledge:

Our star is single and yet it is double. Know how to distinguish its true imprint from its image and you will observe that it shines

[1] Cf. *Alchimie*, p. 137. Published by J-J. Pauvert, Paris.

with more intensity in the light of day than in the darkness of
night.

This statement corroborates and completes the no less categorical
and solemn one made by Basil Valentine *(Douze Clefs)*:

'Two stars have been granted to man by the Gods, in order to
lead him to the great Wisdom: observe them. Oh man! and follow
their light with constancy, because it is Wisdom.'

Are they not the two stars shown in one of the little alchemical
paintings in the Franciscan convent of Cimiez, accompanied by the
Latin inscription expressing the saving virtue inherent in the night
shining of the star?:

'Cum luce salutem; with light, salvation.'

At any rate, if you have even the slightest philosophic sense and
take the trouble to meditate on the words of the undoubted Adepts
quoted above, you will have the key with which Cyliani unlocks the
door of the temple. But if you do not understand, then read the
words of Fulcanelli again and do not go looking elsewhere for a
teaching, which no other book could give so precisely.

There are, then, two stars which, improbable as it may seem, are
really only one star. The star shining on the mystic Virgin—who is
at one and the same time *our mother (mère)* and the *hermetic sea*
(mer)—announces the conception and is but the reflection of that
other, which precedes the miraculous advent of the Son. For
though the celestial Virgin is also called *stella matutina*, the *morning*
star; though it is possible to see on her the splendour of a divine
mark; though the recognition of this source of blessings brings joy
to the heart of the artist; yet it is no more than a simple image,
reflected by the *mirror of Wisdom*. In spite of its importance and
the space given to it by the authors, this visible but intangible star
bears witness to that other, which crowned the divine Child at his
birth. The star which led the Magi to the cave at Bethlehem, as
St. Chrysostom tells us, came to rest, before dispersing, on the
Saviour's head and surrounded him with luminous glory.

I will stress this point, although I am sure that few will thank me
for it: we are truly concerned with a nocturnal star, whose light
shines without great brightness at the pole of the *hermetic sky*. It is,

therefore, important, without allowing oneself to be led astray by appearances, to enquire about this *terrestial sky* mentioned by Vinceslas Lavinius of Moravia and dwelt on at length by Jacobus Tollius:

'You will have understood what this *Sky* is, from the following little commentary of mine and by which the *alchemical sky will have been disclosed*. For:

'This sky is immense and clothes the fields in purple light,
'In which one has recognised one's stars and one's sun.'

It is essential to consider well that the sky and the earth, although they are confused in the original cosmic Chaos, differ neither in substance nor in essence, but become different in quality, quantity and virtue. Does not the alchemical earth, which is chaotic, inert and sterile, contain nevertheless the philosophic sky? Would it then be impossible for the artist, the imitator of Nature and of the divine Great Work, with the help of the secret fire and the universal spirit, to separate in his *little world* the luminous, clear, crystalline parts from the dark, coarse and dense parts? Further, this separation must be made, consisting in the extraction of light from darkness and accomplishing the work of the first of the *Great Days of Solomon*. It is by means of this process that we are able to know what the *philosophic earth* is and what the Adepts have named the *sky of the wise*.

Philalethes, who in his *Entrée ouverte au Palais fermé du Roi* has dealt at greatest length on the practice of the Work, mentions the hermetic star and infers the cosmic magic of its appearance.

'It is the miracle of the world, the assembly of superior virtues in the inferior ones. That is why the Almighty has marked it with an extraordinary sign. The Wise Men saw it in the east, were struck with amazement and knew at once that a King most pure had been born into the the world.

'As for you, as soon as you see his star, follow it to the Cradle, where you will see the lovely Child.'

Then the Adept reveals the manner of operating:

'Let four parts be taken of our fiery dragon, which hides our magic steel in its belly, and nine parts of our lodestone; mix them together, by burning Vulcan, in the form of mineral water, on which a scum will float which must be removed. Throw away the crust, take the inner part, purge three times, by fire and by salt, which will be done easily if Saturn has seen his image in the mirror of Mars.'

Finally Philalethes adds:

'And the Almighty sets his royal seal on the Work and adorns it specially therewith.'

The star is not truly a sign peculiar to the labour of the Great Work. It may be met with in a number of alchemical combinations, special procedures and spagyric operations of comparatively little importance. Nevertheless, it always has the same meaning, showing the partial or total transformation of the bodies on which it is fixed. A typical example is given us by Johann Friedrich Helvetius in an extract from his *Golden Calf (Vitulus Aureus)* which I translate:

'A certain goldsmith of La Hay (whose name is Grillus), a practised disciple of alchemy, but a very poor man according to the nature of this science, some years ago[2] asked my greatest friend, that is to say Johann Kaspar Knottner the dyer of cloths, for some spirits of salt prepared not in the ordinary manner. When Knottner asked whether this special spirits of salt was to be used for metals or not, Gril replied for metals. He then poured this spirits of salt on some lead, which he had placed in a glass receptacle used for preserves or food. Now, after a period of two weeks, there appeared, floating, a very strange and resplendent silvery Star, as though drawn with a compass by a very skilful artist, whereupon Gril, filled with immense joy, told us that he had already seen the visible star of the Philosophers, which he had probably read about in Basil (Valentine). I, myself, and many other honourable men looked with extreme amazment at this star floating on the spirits of salt, while, at the bottom, the lead remained the colour of ashes and swollen

[2] About 1664, the year of the matchless first edition of the *Vitulus Aureus*.

like a sponge. However, after an interval of seven or nine days, this moisture of the spirits of salt, absorbed by the great heat of the July air, disappeared and the star went down to the bottom and rested on this spongy and earthy lead. This result caused amazement to no small number of witnesses. Finally Gril assayed the part of this same ash-coloured lead which had the star adhering to it and he obtained from one pound of lead twelve ounces of assayed silver and from these two ounces, besides, two ounces of excellent gold.'

This is Helvetius' story. I quote it in order to illustrate the presence of the sign of the star on all the internal modifications of bodies treated philosophically. However, I would not like to be the cause of any fruitless and disappointing work which might be undertaken by some enthusiastic readers, based on the reputation of Helvetius, the probity of the eye-witnesses and, perhaps too, on my constant concern for truth. That is why I draw the attention of those, wishing to repeat the process, to the fact that two essential pieces of data are missing in this account: namely, the exact chemical composition of the hydrochloric acid and the preliminary operations carried out on the metal. No chemist will contradict me when I say that ordinary lead, whatever it may be, will never take on the appearance of pumice stone by being subjected, cold, to the action of muriatic acid. Several preparatory operations are, therefore, necessary to cause the dilation of the metal, to separate out from it the coarsest impurities and its perishable elements, in order to bring it finally, by means of the requisite fermentation, to that state of swelling which obliges it to assume a soft spongy structure, already showing a very marked tendency towards a profound change in its specific properties.

Blaise de Vigenère and Naxagoras, for example, have spoken at length of the expediency of a long preliminary cooking process. For if it is true that common lead is dead—because it has suffered reduction and because, as Basil Valentine says, a great flame will consume a little fire—it is none the less true that the same metal, patiently fed a fiery substance, will be reanimated; will little by little regain its lost activity and, from being an inert chemical mass, will become a living philosophic body.

The reader may be surprised that I have spent so much time on a single point of the Doctrine, even devoting the greater part of this preface to it, and, in so doing, I fear that I may have exceeded the usual aim of writing of this kind. However, it must be obvious how logical it was for me to dilate on this subject which, I maintain, leads us straight into Fulcanelli's text. Indeed, right from the beginning my Master has dwelt on the primary role of the star, this mineral Theophany, which announces with certainty the tangible solution of the great secret concealed in religious buildings. This is the *Mystère des Cathédrales*, the very title of the work which—after the 1926 printing, consisting of only 300 copies—we are bringing out in a second edition, augmented by three drawings by Julien Champagne and by Fulcanelli's original notes, collected just as they were without the least addition or alteration. The latter refer to a very agonizing question, with which the Master was concerned for a long time, and on which I shall say a few words in connection with the *Demeures Philosophales*.

However, if *Le Mystère des Cathédrales* needed any justification, it would be enough to point out that this book has restored to light the phonetic *cabala*, whose principles and application had been completely lost. After this detailed and precise elucidation and after the brief treatment of it, which I gave in connection with the centaur, the man-horse of Plessis-Bourré, in *Deux Logis Alchimiques*, this *mother tongue* need never be confused with the Jewish *Kabbala*. Though never spoken, the *phonetic cabala*, this *forceful idiom*, is easily understood and it is—at least according to Cyrano de Bergerac—the *instinct* or *voice of Nature*. By contrast, the Jewish *Kabbala* is full of transpositions, inversions, substitutions and calculations, as arbitrary as they are abstruse. This is why it is important to distinguish between the two words *cabala* and *kabbala*, in order to use them knowledgeably. Cabala derives from καδάλλης or from the Latin *caballus*, a *horse*; *kabbala* is from the Hebrew *Kabbalah*, which means *tradition*. Finally, figurative meanings like *coterie*, *underhand dealing* or *intrigue*, developed in modern usage by analogy, should be ignored so as to reserve for the noun *cabala* the only significance which can be assured for it. This is the one which Fulcanelli himself confirmed in such a masterly way by

B

rediscovering the lost key to the *Gay Science*, the *Language of the Gods*, the *Language of the Birds*. It is the language with which Jonathan Swift, that strange Dean of St. Patrick's, was thoroughly familiar and which he used with so much knowledge and virtuosity.

Savignies, August 1957.

PREFACE

TO THE AMERICAN EDITION

I purchased my first copy of Fulcanelli's *Le Mystère des Cathe-dralés* from Brotherhood of Life bookstore in 1972. Since that time I have studied and reread this definitive work on words, symbolism and hermetic alchemy many, many times. I consider my introduction to this great book as one of the beacons in my search for light.

To you who now have the privilege of reading this magnificent work for the first time...you stand on the threshold of a unique and never-to-be-forgotten experience in the universe of word and letter. I particularly wish to call to your attention pages 42 and 43. In my opinion, these paragraphs comprise some of the finest occult observations on the 'Traditional Kabbala' which have ever been hidden by the 'Bark' of words.

To you who have had the privilege of reading this book before, as well as those now reading it for the first time...you hold in your hands one of the finest editions of *Le Mystère des Cathedralés* which has yet been published, for all of the 49 fine plates have been positioned in relation to the text for easy reference. As you study Fulcanelli's interpretations it will not be necessary to search for the plate that illustrates the text on that particular page.

To all fellow Argonauts...*Le Mystère des Cathedralés* is certainly a major fragment of the 'Golden Fleece' for which we all search...beware of the Alchemical Dragon and may God guide your steps.

ROY E. THOMPSON, JR.

Albuquerque, New Mexico, 1984

INTRODUCTION BY WALTER LANG

TWO UNIVERSES: the universe of science and the universe of alchemy.

To the scientist, alchemy is a farrago of medieval nonsense which enlightened materialist method has rightly consigned to the discard.

To the alchemist, the scientific universe is no more than an abstraction from a much greater whole.

Behind science, says the alchemist, there is Science. All unsuspected, except by a negligible few in every age, there exists a technology of noumena as superior to the technology of phenomena as a supernova is to a candle flame.

To the alchemist, all the phenomena of the universe are combinations of a single prime energy inaccessible to ordinary senses. Only a minute cross section of the total cosmic spectrum is 'bent' by the senses and so rendered tangible. Science has defined this minute abstraction as its total concern and is therefore condemned to turn endlessly inside a nutshell of its own making, learning ever more and more about less and less.

Since alchemists are popularly regarded as at best deluded and at worst deranged, a claim that alchemy is not only science but Science, not only a religion but Religion, is apt to be dismissed out of hand as derisory.

The scientific standpoint begins by being consistent. Man has certain senses and he has developed extensions of his senses which he calls instruments. So equipped, he investigates the universe around him—and occasionally—the universe inside himself.

As there is no sensory evidence for any other kind of universe, why drag one in? Dragging in hypotheses which are unnecessary to explain encountered facts is an affront to the principle of Occam's Razor and therefore to scientific good sense.

In so far as any discipline is entitled to define its own concerns, this is entirely legitimate. What is not so tenable is to imply that because science has selected one possible universe, the universe of fact, and has been superbly successful in charting it, *no other universe can possibly exist*. Science, to be fair, does not exactly say this but it is very happy to see the implication accepted.

The situation is really the Plato's cave allegory one stage up. In Plato's cave, the shadow men live in a seemingly logical world. To them, a more solid world, and one inhabited by men with real eyesight, is a hypothesis unnecessary to explain the shadow world they live in. The shadow men say in effect: 'We know nothing of this superior world you talk about and we don't want to know. We have our own terms of reference and we find them satisfactory. Please go away.'

This is precisely the attitude of modern materialist science to alchemy: 'In terms of the universe we measure and know, your supposed universe is nonsense. Therefore we have no hesitation in asserting with complete confidence that your ideas are delusional.'

In effect: 'No case, abuse the plaintiff's counsel.'

But is there no case? For some thousands of years, some of the best intellects of all cultures have been occupied with the ideas of alchemy. Weighed solely on statistical probability, does it seem likely that an entirely *imaginary* philosophy should attract ceaseless generations of men?

The impasse is worse than it need be because of an almost accidental factor. Alchemy, so far as science has heard, is concerned with making gold and such an activity is so associated with human credulity, cupidity and unscience generally that ordinary philosophy begs to be excused from involvement in anything so obviously puerile.

Is alchemy concerned with making gold? Only in a specific case within a total situation. Alchemists are concerned with gold in much the same way that Mesmer was concerned with hypnotism. The twentieth century took a single aspect of 'Mesmerism', truncated even that, and used the fragment for its own egoistic ends. It declared that it had investigated Mesmerism, exposed its ridiculous pretentions and rendered what was left 'scientific'.

Goethe has a word for this process:

Wer will was Lebendiges beschreiben und erkennen,
Sucht erst den Geist hinaus zu treiben.
Dann hat er, zwar, die Teile in der Hand,
Fehlt leider nur das geistige Band.

Truly science drives out the spirit from the whole and proudly displays the separate bits. Dead, all dead.

If alchemy isn't gold making, what is it? Wilmshurst has defined it as 'the exact science of the regeneration of the human soul from its present sense-immersed state into the perfection and nobility of that divine condition in which it was originally created'.

However, he immediately goes on to offer a second definition which clearly implies that, as with gold making, soul-making is again only a specific case. By inference, a general theory of alchemy might be ventured. *Alchemy is a total science of energy transformation.*

The action of an Absolute in differentiating a prime-source substance into a phenomenal universe is an operation in alchemy. The creation of galactic matter from energy and the creating of energy from matter is alchemy. God is an alchemist.

The decay of radium into lead with the release of radioactivity is alchemy. Nature is an alchemist.

The explosion of a nuclear bomb is alchemy. The scientist is now an alchemist.

All such energy transformations are fraught with great danger and the secrecy which has always surrounded Hermeticism is concerned with this aspect among others.

Nuclear energy was undoubtedly foreseen thousands of years ago. Chinese alchemists are said to have told their pupils that not even a fly on the wall should be allowed to witness an operation. 'Woe unto the world,' they said, 'if the military ever learn the Great Secret.'

The Military *have* learned the great secret—or at any rate one specific aspect of it—and woe indeed to the world, for in the arrogant alchemy of nuclear science there is no place for Goethe's *geistiges Band*.

But if it has taken Western technology so long to uncover a single aspect of the subject, how is it that Bronze Age Egypt and Pythagorean Greece reputedly knew the whole science? Here even the most guarded speculation must seem outrageous.

Materialist science is content—or was until very recently—to suppose that life began as an accident and that once the accident happened, all subsequent steps in evolution would, or at any rate *could*, follow as the mechanical consequence of the factors initially and subsequently present. Perhaps the process was improbable but it was possible.

Recent consideration however, appears to show that by its intrinsic nature, chance expressly *excludes* such a possibility.

For evolution to take place, there is required at every step a shift away from less-organization towards more-organization. The mechanistic view asserts that this enhancement of organization, this negative entropy, could be progressively established from the mechanical consolidation of 'favourable' variations. Recent work in applying mathematical theory to biology suggests that there is a very big hole indeed in this particular bucket.

Even if an increase in order arises fortuitously, this accidental shift must survive if it is to be built upon by the next similar accident. But its survival is by no means assured. Indeed it appears to be vulnerable to collapse in *proportion to its achievement.*

Even in the case of primitive life forms and certainly in higher life forms, the number of possible combinations present at every stage is enormous—so enormous as to require that *entropy must always increase* at the expense of chance arisings in the contrary direction.[1]

Statistically, evolution could not happen. As it demonstrably did happen, it must have done so not merely against probability but actually against the possibilities present in a closed system. The conclusion seems unavoidable: the evolutionary process was not a closed system.

By extension, evolution and its present end-product, man, must have been contrived by forces outside the system (the biosphere) in which it occurred. Such an operation, involving the conscious manipulation of energy levels, may be taken as an operation in alchemy.

Whether the 'artist' who accomplished this great work was a single Intelligence or a consortium of Intelligences seems immaterial: but the myths and classical traditions of demigods is in the highest degree suggestive.

If it is an acceptable proposition that man was the result of a carefully contrived alchemical operation by Higher Powers is it not at least possible that he was given, in addition to consciousness, an insight into the transformation technique that produced him? On

[1] The difficulties inherent in any theory of 'fortuitous' evolution have been indicated by a number of distinguished specialists, among them Professor H. E. Blum (*Form and Structure in Science*, 1964 and in *Nature* Vol. 206, 1965) and by Maurice Vernet (*The Great Illusion of Teilhard de Chardin*). The mathematical and philosophical arguments against the arising of man by the accumulation of accidental increases in order—that is, by mechanical evolution—are developed with great power by J. G. Bennett in *The Dramatic Universe* (London 1966). These arguments contribute to his unified theory in which man is seen as the work of high (but limited) Intelligences.

this assumption, modern man might have, in his own subconscious, fragmentary data which exceptional individuals could recover and assemble into a technology of alchemy. Inevitably such men would be aware of other men who had made the same immense leap and such groups would combine to create schools of alchemy.

There are other theories. One of the most arcane of human traditions suggests that the humanity of our Adam was not the earth's first human race. Some very advanced alchemists have hinted at a range of previous humanities in excess of thirty. If this is the true but wholly unsuspected history of our planet, much knowledge may have been selectively accumulated in a span of existence which imagination is inadequate even to visualize.

At each successive apocalypse, an ark would go out, encapsuling not only the germ plasm necessary to found the next humanity but with it also, some vehicle, some psychological micro-dot, containing the totality of accumulated knowledge.

On this assumption the technique of alchemy would have reached us as a transmission from ancestors whose existence we do not even suspect.

A third possibility is that the Master Alchemists who made man in a solar laboratory have an interest in yet another transformation: the alchemization of man into planetary spirit. Their work may not yet be done. On this assumption, isolated scraps of suitable material would from time to time be selected for further processing in a solar alembic.

The base metal in this case would consist of exceptional human beings and since they would be at the level of incipient conscious energy, they would co-operate in their own transformation.

Whether any, or a combination of all these possibilities is the explanation of the presence of alchemy throughout human history, it is clear that alchemy existed at the dawn of the human story we know.

The material of the Egyptian *Book of the Dead* was said to be old already when it was assembled by Semti in the First Dynasty some five thousand years ago.

Perhaps due to the second law of thermodynamics (which may be as relevant in biology and psychology as it is in dynamics) the evolutionary ferment of Egyptian alchemy began to involve. Maybe the mechanism of its degeneration was a shift in the level of will from which it proceeded. An evolutionary technique would thus become increasingly enlisted for involutionary ends. Alchemy, God-orientated, would become magic, self-dedicated. Such would be the dying Egypt against which Moses inveighed.

As always, however, knowledge of the technique was com-pressed; a torch was lit; an ark was launched. Before Egypt became totally submerged in idolatry the Great Secret was transmitted.

The seeds of alchemy were scattered. Some fell on good ground and flourished; some fell on stony ground and died.

Egypt seems to have sown chiefly in Greece and Israel, perhaps also in China.

Strange as the idea may be, Greece appears to have made less of her chances than she might. The Glory That Was Greece may have been a poor shadow of the Glory That Might Have Been.

Also, Greece stood to Rome as parent to offspring, and Rome proved to be a delinquent child and a degenerate adult in the com-munity of human cultures. The plant of alchemy flowered only briefly in Greece and the seeds that blew to Rome never germinated at all.

The transmission from Egypt to Israel was initially one of great promise but again the promise was not realized. Whether wilting of the plant in Israel was due to the Dispersion or whether the Disper-sion was a consequence of the Jewish failure to manage their alchemical inheritance, is not known. The Elders of Jewry at any rate were unable to find conditions within which their inheritance could be brought to its full actualization.

To ensure its survival in some measure, they were obliged to compromise dangerously. They externalized some of it in the Zohar and maintained a small initiated inner circle. It may be that this circle, very greatly depleted, survived in Europe in isolated pockets like Cracow until the thirties of the present century.

While Greece sowed abortively in Rome during her lifetime, she also sowed posthumously—and successfully in Arabia. Here the alchemical energy chanelled through the esoteric schools of Islam and through exceptional individuals like Jabir externalized in the veritable explosion of Mohammedan art and science of the eighth to twelfth centuries.

The wave of Islam's expansion reached Spain where two streams appear to have joined up. In Seville and Granada there were initiated Jews who carried the Egyptian transmission. They met Arab initiates who carried the Greek transmission and the latter were perhaps reinforced from a permanent powerhouse from which all evolutionary operations are directed.

If it is true that some 'beads of mercury' were reunited through Mohammed, two more were reunited in Spain. Out of this confluence grew a very large part of the whole of Western civilization which we have inherited and whose origin hardly one man in a million has ever suspected in seven centuries.

The current which flowed from the beads of mercury which were reunited in Spain flowed into an immense invisible force field over Europe. The nature of this noumenal structure can never be glimpsed and its functions in a higher dimension cannot even be imagined. It externalized into the common life in a series of culture components which in aggregate constitute a large part of Western civilization.

A selection of these factors at random would include the Christian pilgrimage (based on the form established by the Cluniacs to St. James of Compostella); the Crusades; Heraldry; the orders of chivalry (cheval-ry: from the horse as a glyph of the alchemical 'volatile'?); castle architecture; the Gothic cathedrals; illumination and embroidery; the Troubadours, Albigenses, Cathars and Minnesänger; the Courtly Romances; the Arthurian Quest Theme (reuniting the Celtic pre-Christian Grail Quest); the Cult of the Virgin in Catholicism; the theological philosophy of Albertus Magnus and St. Thomas Aquinas; the cosmology of Bacon; the devotional systems of St. Francis, St. John of the Cross and St. Teresa; the Wandering Players, Jester, harlequinades and Mystery Plays; specialized dancing; falconry and certain ball games; Freemasonry and Rosicrucianism; gardening (the Spanish Gardens); playing cards; the Language of the Birds concept; the Craft Guilds; archery; some medicine like immunology (Paracelsus) and homoeopathy; and cybernetics (Raymond Lully).

All the foregoing were the externalized forms of a major alchemical operation at an invisible level. Only one aspect however, that of *chemical* alchemy, used the terminology which has been subsequently identified with the word.

For some hundreds of years alchemy existed in Europe as a real science of transformation at many levels. At one level it was concerned with the ultimate transformation of human souls.

Perhaps because Christianity had rejected the wisdom component of its total revelation—a decision in which Constantine was probably crucial—alchemy, being concerned with the totality, had to operate in disguise. Precisely because orthodox religion was defective in the wisdom component, any modality which contained it was, *ipso facto*, heresy.

The genuine Christian alchemists—estimated to number four thousand between 1200 and 1656—readopted a chemical code which had served in similar circumstances in the past. A certain principle of nature (rendered in the codex attributed to Hermes, 'as above, so below') ensured that the alchemical process at its hidden level could be represented with full integrity by the terminology of a lower discipline. This lower discipline—metallic chemistry—was all that the common life of Europe ever understood by the word alchemy.

Since Jung's work in alchemy began to infiltrate modern psychology, alchemy as a 'mental' or at any rate a non-physical process, has become a fashionable acceptance. Typical of the 'reductionist' attitudes of the twentieth century is the current belief that alchemy has now been explained. It is 'nothing but' an early and crude study of psychology and perhaps of ESP. Dazzled by the success of science in providing a label for everything, few have bothered to inquire whether the aphorism of Hermes 'as above, so below' might not require a process valid at mental level to be equally valid at physical level.

A label has been affixed, and therefore the mystery is no more. No-one, it seems, notices any conflict between the Jungian 'psychological interpretation' and the documented historical record of men like Helvetius and the Cosmopolite (Alexander Seton?) who demonstrably did make tangible yellow twenty-two carat gold. 'That which is above is as that which is below' might never have been written.

Throughout the whole European record of Alchemy, its genuine practitioners appear to have been under certain obligations which may in fact apply to 'artists' in the Work of every age. It seems that they are required to leave behind them some thread which those who come after may use as a guide line across the web of Ariadne. The indications provided must be in code and the code must be self cancelling; that is, an inquirer who does not possess the first secret must be infallibly prevented from discovering the second. 'Unto him that hath . . .' is nowhere better exemplified than in the attempt to study alchemical texts.

Given that the inquirer knows the first secret, search and unceasing labour may wrest from the code, the next step following but the searcher will need to have made progress in his own personal practice before he is able to unravel a further step. Thus the secret protects itself.

In the course of his work the alchemist may come to understand that certain familiar legends have a wholly new, practical and unsuspected meaning. He may suddenly discover what Abraham was required to sacrifice and why; what the star in the East really heralds; what the Cross may symbolize; and why the veil of the Temple was rent.

The strictly alchemical aspect of The Great Work has been quiescent in Europe for about three centuries but rare and exceptional individuals still find their way through the maze—perhaps by making contact with a source outside Europe—and achieve one or other of the degrees of the Magnum Opus.

Few such instances come to the knowledge of the outside world but one exception to the general rule is the case of the modern alchemist who has come to be known as Fulcanelli.

In the early 'twenties, a French student of alchemy, Eugene Canseliet was studying under the man now known as Fulcanelli. One day the latter charged Canseliet with the task of publishing a manuscript—and then disappeared.

The manuscript was the now famous *Mystère des Cathédrales* and its publication caused a sensation in esoteric circles in Europe.

From internal evidence the author was a man who had either completed, or was on the brink of completing, the Magnum Opus. Interest in such an individual, among those who knew what was involved, was enormous.

For nearly half a century, painstaking research has gone on in an effort to trace the vanished Master. Repeated attempts by private individuals to pick up the trail—and on at least one occasion by an international Intelligence agency—have all ended in a blank wall of silence.

To most, the conclusion seemed inescapable: Fulcanelli, if he ever existed, must be dead.

One man knew better—Fulcanelli's former pupil Canseliet. After a lapse of many years, Canseliet received a message from the alchemist and met him at a pre-arranged rendezvous. The reunion was brief for Fulcanelli once again severed contact and once again disappeared without leaving a trace of his whereabouts.

One circumstance of the reunion was very remarkable—and in an alchemical sense of the highest significance. *Fulcanelli had grown younger*. Canseliet has told the present writer: 'The Master' (when Canseliet had worked with him) 'was already a very old man but he carried his eighty years lightly. Thirty years later, I was to see him again, as I have mentioned, and he appeared to be a man of fifty. That is to say, he appeared to be no older than I was myself'.

One other possible appearance of the mysterious master alchemist is reported by the French researcher Jacques Bergier.

While working as assistant to André Helbronner, the noted physicist who was later to be killed by the Nazis, Bergier was approached one day by an impressive individual who asked Bergier to pass on to Helbronner a strange—and highly knowledgeable— warning. This was to the effect that orthodox science was on the brink of manipulating nuclear energy.

The stranger said it was his duty to warn that this same abyss had been crossed by humanity in the past with disastrous consequences. Knowing human nature, he had no hope that such a warning would have any effect but it was his duty to give it. The mysterious stranger then left. Bergier is convinced to this day that he was in the presence of Fulcanelli.

Treatises have been written to prove that Fulcanelli was a member of the former French Royal Family, the Valois; that he was the painter Julien Champagne; that he was this or that occultist.

Not a few were driven to the conclusion that Fulcanelli was a myth and that no such person had ever existed. This theory is a little difficult to sustain in view of the existence of *Mystère des Cathédrales*. This work is authoritatively accepted as the work of a man who had gone far—very far—in the *practice* of alchemy.

The myth theory is also untenable against the testimony of Canseliet. In September 1922, in a laboratory at Sarcelles and in the presence of the painter Julien Champagne and the chemist Gaston Sauvage, Canseliet himself made an alchemical transmutation of 100 grammes of gold using a minute quantity of the Powder of Projection given to him by his teacher. Thus there is a European, alive at the present time, who personally testifies not only to the existence of Fulcanelli but to the veridical nature of an event which modern science regards as an absurd myth. Legend has it that this transmutation took place 'in a gasworks'. The account seems the plainest possible statement of a purely physical event. Alchemist however, warn repeatedly that when their descriptions seem plainest the camouflage factor is highest. The alerted reader will certainly consider here that a gasworks is a site where a volatile substance is produced from a heavy mineral and will recall that alchemy is a process of 'separating the fine from the gross'.

In being allowed to perform an alchemical operation with energy lent him by another, Canseliet thus joins a remarkable band of privileged—and perhaps bewildered—people who through history have recorded the same experience. These include Johann Schweitzer (whose experience was investigated by Spinoza) Professor Dienheim of Fribourg in 1602 and Christian II Elector of Saxony, in the following year.

But for all practical purposes Fulcanelli has vanished as though he never existed. Only his contributions to the literature of alchemy remains, *Mystère des Cathédrales*.

It has long been believed that the Gothic cathedrals were secret textbooks of some hidden knowledge; that behind the gargoyles and the glyphs, the rose windows and the flying buttresses, a mighty secret lay, all but openly displayed.

This is no longer a theory. Given that the reader of *Mystère des Cathédrales* has even begun to suspect the first secret, Fulcanelli's legacy is at once seen as an exposition of an incredible fact: that, wholly unsuspected by the profane, the Gothic cathedrals have for seven hundred years offered European man a course of instruction in his own possible evolution.

About one thing it seems impossible to have any doubt. The unknown who wrote *Mystère des Cathédrales* KNEW. Fulcanelli speaks as one having authority. By pointing to a glyph in Notre Dame or a statue in Amiens and relating an unknown sculptor's work to some ancient or modern text, Fulcanelli is indicating the steps in a process *he has himself been through*.

Like all who truly KNEW, from Hermes through Geber and the Greek and Arab artists to Lully, Paracelsus and Flamel, Fulcanelli masks and reveals in equal measure and like all before him, he is wholly silent on the *initial step* of the practice.

But in his method of repeatedly underlining certain words and perhaps in some curious sentences on the rose windows, he suggests, as explicitly as he dares, the mightiest secret that man may ever discover.

'Behold,' said Boehme, 'he will show it to you plain enough if you be a Magus and worthy, else you shall remain blind still.'

Le Mystère
des Cathédrales

1

The strongest impression of my early childhood—I was seven years old—an impression of which I still retain a vivid memory, was the emotion aroused in my young heart by the sight of a gothic cathedral. I was immediately enraptured by it. I was in an ecstasy, struck with wonder, unable to tear myself away from the attraction of the marvellous, from the magic of such splendour, such immensity, such intoxication expressed by this more divine than human work.

Since then, the vision has been transformed, but the original impression remains. And if custom has modified the spontaneous and moving character of my first contact, I have never acquired a defence against a sort of rapture when faced with those beautiful picture books erected in our closes and raising to heaven their pages of sculptured stone.

In what language, by what means, could I express my admiration? How could I show my gratitude to those silent masterpieces, those masters without words and without voice? How could I show the thankfulness which fills my heart for everything they have taught me to appreciate, to recognize and to discover?

Without words and without voice? What am I saying! If those stone books have their sculptured letters—their phrases in bas-relief and their thoughts in pointed arches—nevertheless they speak also through the imperishable spirit which breathes from their pages. They are clearer than their younger brothers—the manuscripts and printed books. They have the advantage over them in being translateable only in a single, absolute sense. It is simple in expression, naïve and picturesque in interpretation; a sense purged of subtleties, of allusions, of literary ambiguities.

'The language of stones, spoken by this new art,' as J. F. Colfs[1] says with much truth 'is at the same time clear and sublime, speaking alike to the humblest and to the most cultured heart.' What a moving language it is, this gothic of the stones! A language so moving, indeed, that the songs of Orlando, de Lassus or Palestrina, the organ music of Handel or Frescobaldi, the orchestral works of Beethoven or Cherubini, or, which is greater than all these, the simple and severe Gregorian chant, perhaps the only real chant there is, do nothing but add to the emotions, which the cathedral itself has already aroused. Woe to those who do not like gothic architecture, or at least let us pity them as those who are without heart.

The gothic cathedral, that sanctuary of the Tradition, Science and Art, should not be regardèd as a work dedicated solely to the glory of Christianity, but rather as a vast concretion of ideas, of tendencies, of popular beliefs; a perfect whole, to which we can refer without fear, whenever we would penetrate the religious, secular, philosophic or social thoughts of our ancestors.

[1] J. F. Colfs, *La Filiation généalogique de toutes les Ecoles gothiques*. Paris, Baudry, 1884.

The bold vaulting, the nobility of form, the grandeur of the proportions and the beauty of the execution combine to make a cathedral an original work of incomparable harmony; but not one, it seems, concerned entirely with religious observance.

If the tranquility in the ghostly, multi-coloured light from the tall stained-glass windows and the silence combine as an invitation to prayer, predisposing us to meditation; the trappings, on the other hand, the structure and the ornamentation, in their extraordinary power, release and reflect less edifying sensations, a more secular and, quite bluntly, an almost pagan spirit. Beside the fervent inspiration, born of a strong faith, the thousand and one pre-occupations of the great heart of the people can be discerned there, the declaration of its conscience, of its will, the reflection of its thought at its most complex, abstract, essential and autocratic.

If people go to the building to take part in religious services, if they enter it following a funeral cortège or the joyful procession of a high festival, they also throng there in many other circumstances. Political meetings are held there under the aegis of the bishop; the price of grain and livestock is discussed there; the drapers fix the price of their cloth there; people hurry there to seek comfort, to ask for advice, to beg for pardon. There is scarcely a guild which does not use the cathedral for the passing-out ceremony of its new journeyman, scarcely a guild which does not meet there once a year under the protection of its patron saint.

During the great medieval period it was the scene of other ceremonies, very popular with the masses. There was the *Feast of Fools*—or of the Wise—a processional hermetic fair, which used to set out from the church with its pope, its dignitaries, its enthusiasts and its crowds, the common people of the Middle Ages, noisy, frolicsome, jocular, bursting with vitality, enthusiasm and spirit, and spread through the town. . . . What a comedy it all was, with an ignorant clergy thus subjected to the authority of the *disguised Science* and crushed under the weight of undeniable superiority. Ah! the Feast of Fools, with its *triumphal chariot of Bacchus*, drawn by a male and a female centuar, naked as the god himself, and accompanied by the great Pan; an obscene carnival taking possession of a sacred building; nymphs and naiads emerging

from the bath; gods of Olympus minus their clouds and minus
their clothes; Juno, Diana, Venus and Latona converging on a
cathedral to hear Mass. And what a Mass! It was composed by the
initiate Pierre de Corbeil, Archbishop of Sens, and modelled on a
pagan rite. Here a congregation of the year 1220 uttered the
bacchanal cry of joy: Evoe! Evoe!—and scholars in ecstasy
replied:

> *Haec est clara dies clararum clara dierum!*
> *Haec est festa dies festarum festa dierum![2]*

There was also the *Feast of the Donkey*, almost as gaudy as the
one just mentioned, with the triumphal entry under the sacred
archway of *Master Aliboron*, whose hoof (sabot) once trod the
streets of Jerusalem. Thus our glorious Christ-bearer was celebrated
in a special service, which praised him, in words recalling the
epistle, as *this asinine power, which was worth to the Church the
gold of Arabia, the incense and the myrrh of the land of Saba.*
The priest, being unable to understand this grotesque parody, had
to accept it in silence, his head bent under the ridicule poured out
by these *mystifiers of the land of Saba* or *Caba*, that is the cabalists
themselves. Confirmation of these curious celebrations is to be
found graven by the chisels of the master *image-makers* of the time.
Indeed Witkowski[3] writes that in the nave of Notre-Dame of
Strasbourg 'the bas-relief on one of the capitals of the great pillars
represents a satirical procession, in which a pig may be seen carrying
a holy stoup, followed by donkeys dressed in priestly clothes and
monkeys bearing various religious attributes, together with a fox
enclosed in a shrine. It is the *Procession of the Fox* or the *Feast of
the Donkey*. We may add that an identical scene is illuminated in
folio 40 of manuscript no. 5055 in the Bibliothèque nationale.

Finally there were some bizarre events in which a hermetic
meaning, often a very precise one, was discernible. These were held
every year, with the Gothic church as their theatre. Examples

---

[2] This day is the celebrated day of celebrated days!
This day is the feast day of feast days!

[3] G. J. Witkowski, *L'Art profane à l'Eglise*. Etranger. Paris, Schemit,
1908, p. 35.

include the *Flagellation of the Alleluia*, in which the choirboys energetically whipped their humming-tops (*sabots*)[4] down the aisles of the cathedral of Langres; the *Procession of the Shrovetide Carnival*; the *Devilry of Chaumont*; the procession and banquets of the *Infanterie dijonnaise?* The latter was the last echo of the Feast of Fools, with its *Mad Mother*, its bawdy diplomas, its banner on which two brothers, head to foot, delighted in uncovering *their buttocks*. Until 1538, when the custom died out, a strange *Ball Game* was played inside Saint-Etienne, the cathedral of Auxerre.

2

The cathedral was the hospitable refuge of all unfortunates. The sick, who came to Notre-Dame in Paris to pray to God for relief from their sufferings, used to stay on till they were cured. They were allotted a chapel lit by six lamps near the second door and there they spent the night. There the doctors would give their consultations round the holy-water stoup at the very entrance to the basilica. It was there too that the Faculty of Medicine, which left the University in the thirteenth century to continue independently, gave lectures. This continued to be the custom until 1454, when its last meeting took place, presided over by Jacques Desparts.

The cathedral is the inviolable sanctuary of the hunted and the burial place of the illustrious dead. It is the city within a city, the intellectual and moral centre, the heart of public activity, the apotheosis of thought, knowledge and art.

This host of bristling monsters, of grotesques and comic figures, of masks, of menacing gargoyles, dragons, vampires and tarasques, all these were the secular guardians of an ancestral patrimony. Here

[4] Top with the outline of a *Tau* or *Cross*. In cabalistic language, *sabot* is the equivalent of *cabot* or *chabot*, the *chat botté* (Puss-in-Boots) of the *Tales of Mother Goose*. The Epiphany cake sometimes contains a *sabot* instead of a bean.

art and science, formerly concentrated in the great monasteries, have emerged from their seclusion and colonized the cathedral. They cling to the steeples, to the pinnacles, to the flying buttresses. They hang from the coving, fill the niches. They transform the windows into precious stones and endow the bells with sonorous vibrations. They expand on the church front into a glorious explosion of liberty and expression. Nothing could be more secular than the exotericism of this teaching; nothing more human than this profusion of quaint images, alive, free, animated and picturesque, sometimes in disorder but always vivid with interest. There is nothing more moving than these multiple witnesses to the daily life, the taste, the ideals, the instincts of our fathers. Above all there is nothing more captivating than the sybolism of the ancient alchemists, so ably translated by these modest medieval statues. In this connection Notre Dame of Paris, the Philosophers' church, is indisputably one of the most perfect specimens and, as Victor Hugo said, 'the most satisfying summary of the hermetic science, of which the church of Saint-Jacques-la-Boucherie was such a complete hieroglyph.'

The alchemists of the fourteenth century used to meet there once a week on the day of Saturn, either at the main porch, at the Portal of St. Marcel or else at the little Porte-Rouge, all decorated with salamanders. Denys Zachaire tells us that this custom was followed until the year 1539 'on sundays and feast days'. Noel du Fail says that 'the great place for those academy meetings was Notre-Dame of Paris.'[5]

There, amid a dazzling array of painted and gilded[6] arches, of string-courses and copings, of tympana with multi-coloured figures,

[5] Noel du Fail, *Propos rustiques, baliverneries, contes et discours d'Eutrapel* (ch. x). Paris, Gosselin, 1842.
[6] In the cathedrals everything was gilded and painted in vivid colours. As proof of this we have the words of Martyrius, the fifteenth century Armenian bishop and traveller. This author says that the porch of Notre-Dame of Paris was as resplendent as the gates of Paradise. Purple, rose, azure, silver and gold were to be seen there. Traces of gilding may still be seen at the top of the tympanum of the great portal. The one at the church of Saint-Germain-l'Auxerrois has preserved its painting and its blue vault, starred with gold.

each philosopher would show the result of his labours and work out the next sequence of his researches.

It was there that they assessed probabilities and discussed possibilities and studied on the spot the allegory of the Great Book. Not the least animated part of these gatherings was the abstruse explanation of the mysterious symbols all around them.

In the steps of Gobineau de Montluisant, Cambriel and all the rest, we shall undertake the pious pilgrimage, speak to the stones and question them. Alas! It is almost too late. The vandalism of Soufflot has to a large extent destroyed what the Souffleurs[7] could admire in the sixteenth century. And if art owes some gratitude to those eminent architects Toussaint, Geffroy Dechaume, Boeswillwald, Viollet-le-Duc and Lassus, who restored the basilica so odiously profaned, Science will never again find what it has lost.

However that may be, and in spite of these regrettable mutilations, the motifs still extant are sufficiently numerous to repay the time and trouble of a visit. Indeed I shall consider myself satisfied and amply rewarded if I have been able to awaken the curiosity of the reader, to hold the attention of the shrewd observer and to show to lovers of the occult that it is not impossible even now to rediscover the meaning of the secrets hidden under the petrified exterior of this wondrous book of magic.

3

First of all it is necessary for me to say a word about the term *gothic* as applied to French art, which imposed its rules on all the productions of the Middle Ages and whose influence extends from the twelfth to the fifteenth century.

Some have claimed—wrongly—that it came from the *Goths*, the ancient Germanic people. Others alleged that the word, suggesting something barbarous, was bestowed in derision on a form of art,

[7] Souffleurs = 'puffers', vernacular word for alchemists, from the need to puff at their furnaces—*translator's note*.

whose originality and extreme peculiarity were shocking to the
people of the seventeenth and eighteenth centuries. Such is the
opinion of the classical school, imbued with the decadent principles
of the Renaissance. But truth, preserved in the speech of the common
people, has ensured the continued use of the expression *gothic art*,
in spite of the efforts of the Academy to substitute the term *ogival
art*. There was an obscure reason for this, which should have made
our linguists ponder, since they are always on the look-out for the
derivation of words. How does it come about that so few compilers
of dictionaries have lighted upon the right one? The simple fact is
that the explanation must be sought in the *cabalistic origin* of the
word and not in its *literal root*.

Some discerning and less superficial authors, struck by the
similarity between *gothic* (gothique) and goetic (goetique) have
thought that there must be a close connection between gothic art
and goetic art, i.e. magic.

For me, gothic art (*art gothique*) is simply a corruption of the
word *argotique* (cant), which sounds exactly the same. This is in
conformity with the *phonetic law*, which governs the traditional
cabala in every language and does not pay any attention to spelling.
The cathedral is a work of *art goth* (gothic art) or of *argot*, i.e. cant
or slang. Moreover, dictionaries define *argot* as 'a language peculiar
to all individuals who wish to communicate their thoughts without
being understood by outsiders'. Thus it certainly is a *spoken cabala*.
The *argotiers*, those who use this language, are the hermetic
descendants of the *argonauts*, who manned the ship *Argo*. They
spoke the *langue argotique*—our *langue verte* ('green language' or
slang)—while they were sailing towards the felicitious shores of
Colchos to win the famous *Golden Fleece*. People still say about
a very intelligent, but rather sly, man: '*he knows everything, he
understands cant.*' All the Initiates expressed themselves in cant;
the vagrants of the *Court of Miracles*—headed by the poet Villon—
as well as the Freemasons of the Middle Ages, 'members of the
lodge of God', who built the *argotique* masterpieces, which we still
admire today. Those constructional sailors (nautes) also knew the
route to the Garden of the Hesperides. . . .

In our day, cant is spoken by the humble people, the poor, the despised, the rebels, calling for liberty and independence, the outlaws, the tramps and the wanderers. Cant is the cursed dialect, banned by high society, by the nobility (who are really so little noble), the well-fed and self-satisfied middle class, luxuriating in the ermine of their ignorance and fatuity. It remains the language of a minority of individuals living outside accepted laws, conventions, customs and etiquette. The term *voyous* (street-arabs) that is to say *voyants* (seers) is applied to them and the even more expressive term *sons or children of the sun*. Gothic art is in fact the *art. got* or *cot* (χο)—*the art of light* or of the spirit.

People think that such things are merely a play on words. I agree. The important thing is that such word-play should guide our faith towards certainty, towards positive and scientific truth, which is the key to the religious mystery, and should not leave us wandering in the capricious maze of our imagination. The fact is that there is neither chance nor coincidence nor accidental correspondence here below. All is foreseen, preordained, regulated; and it is not for us to bend to our pleasure the inscrutable will of Destiny. If the usual sense of words does not allow us any discovery capable of elevating and instructing us, of bringing us nearer to our Creator, then words become useless. The spoken word, which gives man his indisputable superiority, his dominion over every living thing, loses its nobility, its greatness, its beauty. It becomes no more than a distressing vanity. Besides, language, the instrument of the spirit, has a life of its own—even though it is only a reflection of the universal Idea. We do not invent anything, we do not create anything. All is in everything. Our microcosm is only an infinitesimal, animated, thinking and more or less imperfect particle of the macrocosm. What we believe we have ourselves discovered by an effort of our intelligence, exists already elsewhere. Faith gives us a presentiment of what this is. Revelation gives us absolute proof. Often we pass by a phenomenon—or a miracle even—without noticing it, like men blind and deaf. What unsuspected marvels we should find, if we knew how to dissect words, to strip them of their bark and liberate the spirit, the divine light which is within! Jesus expressed himself only in parables; can we deny the truth which the parables teach? In present-day conconversation is it not the ambiguities, the approximations, the puns or the assonances which characterize spirited people, who are glad to escape from the tyranny of the letter and thereby—unwittingly—show themselves cabalists in their own right.

Finally I would add that *argot* (cant) is one of the forms derived from the *Language of the Birds*, parent and doyen of all other languages—the one spoken by philosophers and *diplomats*. It was knowledge of this language which Jesus revealed to his Apostles, by sending them his spirit, the Holy Ghost. This is the language which teaches the mystery of things and unveils the most hidden truths. The ancient Incas called it the *Court Language*, because it was used by diplomats. To them it was the key to the *double science*, sacred and profane. In the Middle Ages it was called the *Gay Science* and the *Gay Knowledge*, the *Language of the Gods*, the Dive-Bouteille.[8] Tradition assures us that men spoke it before the building of the *Tower of Babel*, which event caused this sacred language to be perverted and to be totally forgotten by the greater part of humanity. Today, apart from cant, we find its character in a few local dialects, such as Picard, Provençal, etc. and in the language of the gypsies.

Mythology would have it that the famous soothsayer, Tiresias[9] had perfect knowledge of the *Language of the Birds*, which Minerva, goddess of *Wisdom*, revealed to him. He shared it, they say, with Thales of Miletus, Melampus and Appolonius of Tyana,[10] legendary personages, whose names, in the science we are considering, ring eloquently enough to require no analysis from me.

[8] *The Life of Gargantua and Pantagruel* by François Rabelais is an esoteric work, a novel in cant. The good curé of Meudon reveals himself in it as a great initiate, as well as a first-class cabalist.

[9] It is said that Tiresias was deprived of his sight for revealing to mortals the secrets of Olympus. However he lived 'for seven, eight or nine ages of man' and is supposed to have been successively man and woman.

[10] Philosopher, whose life, crammed full of legends, miracles and prodigious deeds, seems to be extremely hypothetical. The name of this semi-fabulous personage seems to me to be just a mytho-hermetic image of the compost or *philosophic rebis*, realized by the union of brother and sister, of Gabritius and Beya, of *Apollo and Diana*. In that case the marvels recounted by Philostratus, being chemical in character, should not surprise us.

4

With rare exceptions, the ground plan of the gothic churches—cathedrals, abbey and collegiate churches—takes the form of a Latin cross laid on the ground. Now, the *cross is the alchemical hieroglyph of the crucible*, which used to be called in French *cruzol*, *crucible* and *croiset* (according to Ducange, the vulgar Latin *crucibulum*, crucible, has as its root *crux, crucis*, a cross).

It is indeed in the crucible that the first matter suffers the Passion, like Christ himself. It is in the crucible that it dies to be revived, purified, spiritualized and transformed. Further, do not the common people, those faithful guardians of the oral tradition, express the human ordeal on earth by religious parables and hermetic similes? —*To bear one's cross, to climb one's Calvary, to go through the crucible* of existence, are all current sayings, in which we find the same sense expressed by the same symbolism.

Let us not forget that around the *luminous cross*, seen in a vision by Constantine, appeared those prophetic words, which he adopted on his standard: *In this sign thou shalt conquer*. Remember too, my brother alchemists, that the cross bears the *imprint of three nails* used to sacrifice the Christ-body: an image of the three purifications by sword and fire. Meditate similarly on that clear passage of St. Augustine in his *Dispute with Tryphon* (Dialogus cum Tryphone 40): 'The mystery of the Lamb which God had ordered to be sacrificed at Easter,' he says, 'was the figure of Christ, with which those who believe stain their abodes, that is to say themselves, by the faith which they have in him. Further, *this lamb*, which the Law prescribed *to have roasted whole*, was the symbol of the cross which Christ had to endure, since the lamb to be roasted is disposed in such a way as to represent a cross. One of the arms of the cross pierces it through and through, from the hind quarters to the head. The other pierces its shoulders and the forefeet (the Greek says: the hands, χεεϛρί) of the lamb are tied to it.'

The cross is a very ancient symbol, used in all ages, in all religions, by all peoples, and one would be wrong to consider it as a special emblem of Christianity, as the Abbé Ansault[11] has more than amply shown. We say further that the ground plan of the great religious buildings of the Middle Ages, by the addition of a semi-circular or elliptical apse joined to the choir, assumes the shape of the Egyptian hieratic sign of the *crux ansata*, the *ankh*, which signifies *universal life* hidden in matter. An example of this may be seen at the museum of St. Germain-en-Laye, on a Christian sarcophagus from the crypts of St. Honoré at Arles. On the other hand, the hermetic equivalent of the ankh symbol is the emblem of Venus or Cypris (in Greek Κυπρις, the impure) i.e. common copper, which some, in order to veil the meaning further, have translated as brass or latten. 'Whiten the latten and burn your books' is the repeated advice of all the good authors. Κυπρος is the same word as Σουφρος, *sulphur*, which has the meaning of manure, muck, dung, ordure. 'The wise man will find our stone even in the dung heap,' writes the Cosmopolite, 'while the ignorant will not be able to believe that it exists in gold.'

It is thus that the ground plan of a Christian building reveals to us the qualities of the first matter, and its preparation by the *sign of the cross*, which points the way for the alchemist to obtain the *First Stone*—the corner stone of the philosophers' Great Work. It is on this *stone* that Jesus built his Church; and the medieval freemasons have symbolically followed the divine example. But before being dressed to serve as a base for the work of gothic art, as well as for the philosophical work of art, the rough, impure, gross and unpolished stone was often given the *image of the devil*.

Notre Dame of Paris possessed a similar hieroglyph, situated under the rood-screen, at the corner of the choir rail. It was a figure of the devil, opening an enormous mouth in which the faithful extinguished their candles. Thus the sculptured block of stone was marked with streaks of candle-grease and blackened with smoke. The common people called this image *Maistre Pierre du Coignet* (Master Peter (stone) of the Corner), which was a continual embarrasment to the archaeologists. Now, this stone, which was intended to represent the first matter of the Work, personified under the aspect

[11] The Abbé Ansault, *La croix avant Jésus-Christ*, Paris, V. Rétaux, 1894.

of *Lucifer (the morning star)*, was the symbol of our *corner stone*, the *headstone of the corner*. The stone which the builders rejected,' writes Amyraut,[12] 'has been made the *headstone of the corner*, on which rests the whole structure of the building; but which is a stumbling-block and stone of shame, against which they dash themselves to their ruin.' As for the dressing of this corner stone—I mean its preparation—it can be seen translated in a very fine bas-relief of the time, sculptured on the outside of the building, on an absidal chapel facing the Rue du Cloître-Notre-Dame.

5

Whilst the decoration of the salient parts was reserved for the *tailleur d'imaiges* (sculptor), the ornamentation of the floor of the cathedrals was assigned to the worker in ceramics. The floor was normally flagged or tiled with baked clay tiles, painted and covered with a lead glaze. In the Middle Ages this art had reached such perfection that historical subjects could be assured of a sufficient variety of design and colour. Use was also made of little cubes of multi-coloured marble, in the manner of the Byzantine mosaics. Among the motifs most frequently employed, one should note the labyrinths, which were traced on the ground at the point of intersection of the nave and the transepts. The churches of Sens, Rheims, Auxerre, St. Quentin, Poitiers and Bayeux have preserved their labyrinths. In the centre of the labyrinth at Amiens a large flagstone used to be visible, encrusted with a bar of gold and a semicircle of the same metal, showing the run rising above the horizon. Later on, the gold sun was replaced by a copper one and the latter in its turn disappeared, never to be replaced at all. As for the labyrinth at Chartres, called in the common tongue La Lieue (the league) for Le Lieu (the place) and drawn on the paving stones of the nave, it is composed of a whole series of concentric circles coiling one within another in endless variety. At the centre of the figure,

[12] M. Amyraut, *Paraphrase de la Première Epître de saint Pierre* (ch. II, v. 7). Saumur, Jean Lesnier, 1646, p. 27.

the combat of Theseus and the Minotaur used to be seen—yet
another proof of the infiltration of pagan themes into Christian
iconography and consequently of an evident mytho-hermetic
meaning. However it is not a matter of establishing any connection
between these images and those famous constructions of antiquity,
the labyrinths of Greece and Rome.

The labyrinth of the cathedrals or the *Labyrinth of Solomon* is,
Marcellin Berthelot[13] tells us, 'a cabalistic figure found at the head
of certain alchemical manuscripts and which is part of the magic
tradition associated with the name of Solomon. It is a series of
concentric circles, interrupted at certain points, so as to form a
bizarre and inextricable path.'

The picture of the labyrinth is thus offered to us as emblematic
of the whole labour of the Work, with its two major difficulties, one
the path which must be taken in order to reach the centre—where the
bitter combat of the two natures takes place—the other the way which
the artist must follow in order to emerge. It is there that the *thread
of Ariadne* becomes necessary for him, if he is not to wander
among the winding paths of the task, unable to extricate himself.

My intention is not to write, as Batsdorff did, a special treatise
on what this *thread of Ariadne* is, which enabled Perseus to fulfil
his purpose. But in laying stress on the cabala, I hope to furnish
shrewd investigators with some precise information on the
symbolical value of the famous myth.

Ariane (Ariadne) is a form of *airagne* (araignée, the spider) by
metathesis of the *i*. In Spanish ñ is pronounced *gn*; αραχυη(the spider)
can thus be read *arahne, arahni, arahagne*. Is not our soul the spider,
which weaves our own body? But this word appears in other forms.
The verb αἱρω means *to take, to seize, to draw, to attract*; whence
αἱρην, that which takes, seizes, attracts. Thus αἱρην is the *lodestone*,
that virtue shut up in the body, which the Wise call their Magnesia.
Let us continue. In Provençal iron is called *aran* and *iran*, according
to the different dialects. This is the masonic *Hiram*, the divine *ram*,
the architect of the *Temple of Solomon*. The félibres[14] called the

[13] *La Grande Encyclopédie*. Art. Labyrinths. T. xxl, p. 703.
[14]*Translator's note:* The félibres were members of a society of writers,
founded in 1854, to preserve the Provençal language.

spider *aragno* and *iragno, airagno*; The Picard version is *aregni*. Compare all that with the Greek Σιδηρος, which may mean either iron or lodestone. Nor is this all. The verb ἀρυω means *the rising of a star from out of the sea*, when αρυαν (Aryan), *the star which rises out of the sea*; or *ariane* is thus the *Orient*, by the permutation of vowels. Further, ἀρυω has also the sense *to attract*; thus αρυαν is also the *lodestone*. If we now compare Σιδηρος, which has given the Latin *sidus, sideris* a *star*, we shall recognize our Provençal *aran, iran, airan*—the Greek αρυαν, *the rising sun*.

Ariadne, the mystic spider, has escaped from Amiens, leaving only the trace of her web on the paving stones of the choir. . . .

Let us recall in passing that the most celebrated of the ancient labyrinths, that of Cnossos in Crete, which was discovered in 1902 by Dr. Evans of Oxford, was called *Absolum*. We would point out that this term is close to the *Absolute*, which is the name by which the ancient alchemists designated the philosophers' stone.

6

All churches have their apse turned towards the south-east, their front towards the north-west, while the transepts, forming the arms of the cross, are directed to the north-east and the south-west. That is the invariable orientation, intended in such a fashion that the faithful and profane, entering the church by the west, walk straight to the sanctuary facing the direction in which the sun rises, i.e. the Orient, Palestine, cradle of Christianity. They leave the shadows and walk towards the light.

As a consequence of this arrangement, one of the three rose windows which adorn the transepts and the main porch, is never lighted by the sun. This is the north rose, which glows on the facade of the left transept. The second one blazes in the midday sun; this is the southern rose, open at the end of the right transept. The last window is lit by the coloured rays of the setting sun. This is the great rose, the porch window, which surpasses its side sisters in size and brilliance. Thus on the façade of a gothic cathedral the

D

colours of the Work unfold in a circular progression, going from the shadows—represented by the absence of light and the colour black —to the perfection of ruddy light, passing through the colour white, considered as being the mean between black and red.

In the Middle Ages, the central rose window of the porches was called *Rota*, the wheel. Now, *the wheel* is the alchemical hieroglyph of the time necessary for the coction of the philosophical matter, and consequently of the coction itself. The sustained, constant and equal fire, which the artist maintains night and day in the course of this operation, is for this reason called the *fire of the wheel*. Moreover, in addition to the heat necessary for the liquefaction of the philosophers' stone, a second agent is needed as well, called the *secret* or *philosophic fire*. It is this latter fire, sustained by ordinary heat, which *makes the wheel turn* and produces the various phenomena which the artist observes *in his vessel*:

> I recommend you to go by this road and no other.
> Only take notice of the tracks of my wheel,
> And, in order to give an equal heat overall,
> Do not rise or descend too soon to heaven or earth.
> For in rising too high you will be burnt by heaven,
> And in descending too low you will be destroyed by earth.
> But if your course remains set in the middle
> The route will be plainer and the way more sure.[15]

Thus the rose alone represents the action of the fire and its duration. That is why the medieval decorators sought in their rose windows to translate the movements of matter, stirred up by the elementary fire, as may be seen on the north portal of Chartres cathedral, in the roses of Toul (St. Gengoult), of St. Antoine of Compiègne, etc. The preponderance of the fiery symbol in the architecture of the fourteenth and fifteenth centuries, which neatly characterizes the last period of medieval art, has given rise to the name *flamboyant gothic* for the style of this period.

[15] De Nuysement, *Poème philosophic de la Vérité de la Phisique Mineralle* in *Traittez de L'Harmonie et Constitution generalle du Vray Sel*. Paris, Périer et Buisard, 1620 and 1621, p. 254.

Some roses, emblematic of a certain compound, have a particular meaning, which underlines still further the properties of this *substance*, which *the Creator has sealed* with his own hand. This *magic seal* reveals to the artist that he has followed the right road and that the philosophical mixture has been prepared according to *canon* law. It is a radiate figure, with six points *(digamma)* called the *Star of the Magi*, which beams on the surface of the compound, that is to say above the crib in which Jesus, the *Child-King*, lies.

Among the buildings which present us with starred roses with six petals—a reproduction of the traditional *Solomon's Seal*,[16] I would mention the cathedral Saint-Jean and the Church of Saint-Bonaventure at Lyons (rose windows of the portals); the Church of Saint-Gengoult at Toul; the two roses of Saint-Vulfran at Abbeville; the Calend Portal at the Cathedral of Rouen; the splendid blue rose of the Sainte-Chapelle, etc.

Since this sign is of the greatest interest to the alchemist—is it not the star which guides him and which announces to him the birth of the Saviour?—it would be useful here to collect certain texts recounting, describing and explaining its appearance. I shall leave to the reader the task of making useful comparisons, of co-ordinating the versions and of picking out the positive truth, which is combined with legendary allegory in these enigmatic fragments.

7

Varro, in his *Antiquitates rerum humanorum*, recalls the legend of Aeneas saving his father and his household gods from the *flames of Troy* and, *after long wanderings*, arriving at the fields of *Laurentum*,[17] the goal of his journey. He gives the following explanation:

Ex quo de Troja est egressus Aeneas, Veneris eum per diem

---

[16] Convallaria polygonata, commonly called *Solomon's Seal*, owes its name to its stem, the section of which is starred like the magic sign attributed to the King of the Israelites, the son of David.

[17] *Laurente* (Laurentium) is cabalistically *l'or enté* (grafted gold).

quotidie stellam vidisse, donec ad agrum Laurentum veniret, in quo eam non vidit ulterius; qua recognovit terras esse fatales.[18] (After his departure from Troy, he saw every day and during the day the *Star of Venus*, until he arrived at the fields of Laurentum, where he ceased to see it. This fact made him realize that these were the *lands allotted by destiny.*)

Here is a legend taken from a work entitled the *Book of Seth* and which a sixth century author relates in these terms:

'I heard some people speaking of a Writing, which, although far from certain, is not contrary to the faith and is rather agreeable to hear. It tells that a race existed in the Far East on the shores of the Ocean, who possessed a book attributed to Seth, which spoke of the future appearance of this star and of the gifts, which should be taken to the Child, which prediction was given as transmitted from father to son by generations of the wise men.

'They chose out twelve from the most learned among them and from those most skilled in the mysteries of the heavens and gave themselves up to waiting for this star. If one of them came to die, his son or a near relative, who was in the same expectation, was chosen to replace him.

'They were called in their tongue *Magi*, because they glorified God *in silence* and in a low voice.

'Every year, after the harvest, these men climbed up on a mountain, which was called in their language the *Mount of Victory*, which enclosed a *cavern hewn out of the rock* and pleasant on account of the streams and trees, which surrounded it. When they arrived at the summit, they washed themselves, prayed and praised God in silence *for three days*; this was their practice *in every generation*, always waiting in case by chance this *star of fortune* should appear during their generation. But finally *it did appear on the Mount of Victory*, in the form of a *little child* and presenting the *shape of a cross*; it spoke to them, *instructed* them and bade them depart for Judaea.

'The star went before them for two years and neither bread nor water was ever lacking on their journey.

'What they did next is reported briefly in the Gospel.'

[18] *Varro* in *Servius, Aeneid*, bk. 111, p. 386.

The shape of the star was different according to this other legend, the age of which is unknown: [19]

'During the journey, which lasted thirteen days, the Magi took neither rest nor food; they did not feel any need, and this period seemed to them not to last more than a day. The nearer they came to Bethlehem, the brighter the star shone. *It had the form of an eagle, flying through the air and moving its wings. Above it was a cross.*'

The following legend, entitled *Some events, which took place in Persia at the time of the birth of Christ,* is attributed to Julius Africanus, a chronicler of the third century, although the actual date of it is unknown.[20]

The scene takes place in Persia in a temple of Juno (Hρής) built by Cyrus. A priest announces that Juno has conceived. All the statues of the gods dance and sing at this news. *A star descends* and announces the birth of a *Child, the Beginning and the End.* All the statues fall down with their faces to the ground. The Magi announce that this Child is born at Bethlehem and advise the king to send ambassadors. Then *Bacchus* (Διονυσος) appears and predicts that this Child will drive out all the false gods. Departure of the Magi, guided by the star. At Bethlehem they greet Mary, have a portrait of her with the Child painted by a skilful slave and place it in their chief temple with this inscription: '*To Jupiter Mithra* (Διί Ηλίω —*to the Sun God) to the Great God, to King Jesus, the Persian Empire makes this dedication*'.

'The light of this star,' writes St. Ignatius,[21] 'surpassed that of all the others; its brilliance was ineffable and its novelty was such that all those who looked at it were struck with astonishment. *The sun, moon and the stars formed a choir round this star.*'

Huginus à Barma, in the *Practice* of his work,[22] uses the same terms to describe the matter of the Great Work, on which the star appears. 'Take some *real earth,*' he says, '*well impregnated with the rays of the sun, the moon and the other stars.*'

---

[19] *Apocryphes*, bk. II, p. 469.
[20] *Julius Africanus*, in *Patr. grecque*, bk. X, p. 97 and 107.
[21] *Epistle to the Ephesians*, ch. XIX.
[22] Huginus à Barma, *La Règne de Saturne changé en Siècle d'or*. Paris, Derieu, 1780.

In the fourth century, the philosopher Chalcidius, who, as Mullachius, the last of his editors, says, taught that the gods of Greece, the gods of Rome and the gods of foreigners should be adored, has preserved a record of the Star of the Magi and the explanation for it given by the wise. After having spoken of a star called *Ahc* by the Egyptians, which announces bad fortune, he adds:

'There is another and more venerable story, which attests that *the rising of a certain star* announced not sickness or death, but the descent of a venerable God, for the grace of conversation with man and for the advantage of mortal affairs. *The wisest* of the Chaldeans, having seen this star while journeying *through the night*, as men perfectly versed in the contemplation of celestial things, sought, it is told, for the *recent birth of a God* and having found the majesty of this Child, they rendered to him the vows fitting to such a great God. *This is much better known to you than to others.*[23]

Diodorus of Tarsus[24] shows himself even more explicit, when he affirms that 'this star was not one of those which people the heavens, but a certain virtue or urano-diurnal (δυναμίς) force (θειοτέραν) *having assumed the form of a star* in order to announce the birth of the Lord among us.

Gospel according to St. Luke, II, v. 8-14:

'And there were in the same country shepherds abiding in the field, keeping watch over their flock by night. And, lo, the angel of the Lord came upon them, and the *glory of the Lord* shone round about them: and they were sore afraid.

'And the angel said unto them, Fear not: for, behold, I bring you *good tidings* of great joy, which shall be to all people. For unto you is born this day in the city of David a Saviour, which is Christ the Lord. And this shall be a *sign* unto you: Ye shall find the babe *wrapped in swaddling clothes, lying in a manger*.

'And suddenly there was with the angel a multitude of the heavenly host praising God and saying, Glory to God in the highest, and on earth peace, good will toward men.'

[23] Chalcidius, *Comm. in Timaeum Platonis*, c. 125; in the *Frag. Philosophorum graecorum* of Didot, bk. II, p. 210.—Chalcidius is obviously speaking to an initiate.

[24] Diodorus of Tarsus, *On Destiny*, in *Photius*, cod. 233; *Patr. greque*, bk. CIII, p. 878.

Gospel according to St. Matthew, II, v. 1–2, v. 7–11.

'Now when Jesus was born in Bethlehem of Judaea in the days of Herod the king, behold, there came wise men from the east to Jerusalem, saying, Where is he that is born King of the Jews? for we have seen his star in the east, and are come to worship him.

'Then Herod, when he had privily called the wise men, enquired of them diligently *what time the star appeared*. And he sent them to Bethlehem, and said, Go and search diligently for the young child: and when ye have found him bring me word again, that I may come and worship him also.

'When they had heard the king, they departed; and, lo, the star, which they saw in the east, went before them, till it came and stood over where the young child was.

'When they saw the star, they rejoiced with exceeding great joy. And when they were come into the house, they saw the young child with Mary his mother, and fell down and worshipped him; and when they had opened their treasures, they presented him with gifts: gold, and frankincense, and myrrh.'

Speaking of such strange happenings and faced with the impossibility of attributing the cause of them to any celestial phenomenon, A. Bonnetty,[25] struck by the mystery which envelops these narratives, asks:

'Who are these Magi and what is one to think of this star? That is what rational critics and others are wondering at this moment. It is difficult to reply to these questions, because ancient and modern Rationalism and Ontologism, drawing all their knowledge from their own resources, have made one forget all the *means by which the ancient peoples of the East preserved their primitive traditions*.'

We find the first reference to the star in the mouth of Balaam. The latter, who is said to have been born in the town of Pethor on the Euphrates, lived, they say, around the year 1477 B.C. at the centre of the rising Assyrian Empire. Balaam, prophet or Mage in Mesopotamia, cries out:

'How shall I curse, whom God hath not cursed? or how shall I defy, whom the Lord hath not defied? . . . I shall see him, but not

[25] A Bonnetty, *Documents historiques sur la Religion des Romains*, bk. II, p. 564.

now: I shall behold him, but not nigh: *there shall come a Star out of Jacob, and a Sceptre shall rise out of Israel. . . .'* (Numbers, XXIII, 8; XXIV, 17).

In symbolic iconography, the star is used to indicate conception, as well as birth. The Virgin is often represented with a nimbus of stars. The Virgin at Larmor (Morbihan) forms part of a fine triptych, representing the death of Christ and the suffering of Mary (Mater dolorosa). In the sky of the central composition can be seen the sun, moon and stars and the scarf of Iris. The Virgin holds in her right hand a large star—*maris stella*—an epithet given to her in a Catholic hymn.

G. J. Witkowski[26] describes for us a very curious stained glass window, which used to be near the sacristy in the old church of Saint-Jean at Rouen, now destroyed. This window showed the *Conception of St. Romain.* 'His father, Benoît, Counsellor of Clothair II, and his mother, Félicité, were lying in a bed, completely naked in accordance with the custom, which lasted until the middle of the sixteenth century. The conception was shown by a star, which shone *on the coverlet* in contact with the belly of the woman. . . . The borders of this window, which was already strange enough on account of its main motif, were ornamented with medallions on which one could see, not without surprise, the figures of *Mars, Jupiter, Venus,* etc. and, so that there should be no doubt about their identity, the figure of each deity was accompanied by its name.'

8

Just as the human soul has its hidden recesses, so the cathedral has its secret passages. They extend underground below the church and, taken all together, they form the crypt (from the Greek Κρυπτός, *hidden*).

In this low, damp, cold place, the observer experiences a strange

[26] G. J. Witkowski, *L'Art profane à l'Eglise.* France, Paris, Schemit, 1908, p. 382.

feeling and one which imposes silence: it is the feeling of power, combined with darkness. We are here in the abode of the dead, as in the basilica of Saint-Denis, burial-place of the famous; as in the Roman catacombs, cemetery of the Christians. Paving stones, marble mausoleums, tombs, historical debris, fragments of the past abound. A heavy silence fills the vaulted space. The thousand outside noises, vain echoes of the world, do not reach us here. Are we about to issue forth into the caves of the cyclops? Are we on the threshold of a Dantean inferno, or beneath the subterranean galleries, so welcoming, so hospitable to the first martyrs? All is mystery, anguish and fear in this obscure retreat.

Around us are numbers of enormous pillars, sometimes in pairs, standing on their broad chamfered bases; short capitals, only slightly projecting, squat and unpretentious; rough, worn shapes, in which elegance and richness give place to solidarity. Thick muscles, contracted under the effort, which untiringly share the formidable weight of the entire building. Nocturnal will, silent, rigid, strained in eternal resistance to being crushed. Material power, which the builder knew how to direct and distribute, by giving to all these members the archaic aspect of a herd of fossilized pachyderms, joined to each other, rounding their bony backs, hollowing their stone chests, under the pressure of an excessive burden. Real, but occult, power, which is exercised in secret, develops in the darkness, toils without respite in the deep foundations of the work. That is the dominant impression, felt by the visitor, when going through the galleries of a gothic crypt.

Formerly the subterranean chambers of the temples served as abodes for the statues of *Isis*, which, at the time of the introduction of Christianity into Gaul, became those *black Virgins*, which the people in our day surround with a quite special veneration. Their symbolism is, moreover, identical; both the one and the other bear the same famous inscription on their base: Virgini pariturae; *to the Virgin about to give birth*. Ch. Bigarne[27] tells us of several statues of Isis, described in the same way. 'Already,' says the learned Pierre Dujols, in his *Bibliographie générale de l'Occulte*, 'the

[27] Ch. Bigarne, *Considérations sur le Culte d'Isis chez les Eduens.* Beaune, 1862.

scholar Elias Schadius, in his book *De dictis Germanicis*, had
pointed out a similar inscription: *Isidi, seu Virgini ex qua filius
proditurus est.*[28] So these icons appear to have none of the Christian
meaning ascribed to them, at any rate exoterically. Isis before
conception is, says Bigarre, in astronomical theogany, that attribute
of the Virgin, which several monuments considerably prior to
Christianity describe under the name of *Virgo paritura*, that is to
say the *earth before its fecundation* and which the rays of the sun
are soon going to bring to life. She is also the mother of the gods,
as is attested by a stone at Die: *Matri deum, magnae ideae'*. The
esoteric meaning of our *black Virgins* cannot better be defined.
They represent in hermetic symbolism the *virgin earth*, which the
artist must choose as the *subject* of his Great Work. It is first matter
in mineral state, as it comes out of the ore-bearing strata, deeply
buried under the rocky mass. It is, the texts tells us, 'a heavy, brittle,
friable *black substance*, which has the appearance of a stone and,
like a stone, can shatter into minute fragments.' Thus it appears to
be the rule that the personified hieroglyph of this mineral possesses
its special colour and that the subterranean parts of temples are
reserved as its dwelling place.

Nowadays, black Virgins are not numerous. I will mention a
few, all of whom enjoy great celebrity. The Cathedral of Chartres
is best endowed in this respect. It has two of them, one, called by
the expressive name of *Notre-Dame-sous-Terre* (Our Lady Underground), in the crypt, is seated on a throne, whose pedestal bears the
inscription mentioned above: *Virgini pariturae*. The other one,
outside, called Notre-Dame-du-Pilier (Our Lady of the Pillar),
occupies the centre of a niche filled with *ex votos*, in the form of
burning hearts. The latter, Witkowski tells us, is the object of
devotion of a great number of pilgrims. 'In early times,' adds this
author, 'the stone column, which supports it, was worn away by the
licks and bites of its fervent worshippers, like the foot of St. Peter in
Rome, or the knee of Hercules, which the heathen worshipped in
Sicily; but, in order to preserve it from too ardent kisses, in 1831 it
was given a wooden surround.' Chartres, with its underground
Virgin, ranks as the most ancient of all the places of pilgrimage. At

[28] To Isis, or to the Virgin from whom the son will be born.

I.   OUR LADY-OF-CONFESSION
Black Virgin of the Crypts of St. Victor, Marseilles.

first it was just an ancient statuette of Isis 'sculpted before Christ' as ancient local chronicles tell. At any rate, our present figure dates only from the very end of the eighteenth century, the one of the goddess Isis having been destroyed at some unknown date and replaced by a wooden statue, in which she holds her child on her lap. This was burnt in 1793.

As for the black Virgin of Notre-Dame of Puy, whose limbs are not visible, she assumes the shape of a triangle, with her high-necked gown falling to her feet without a fold. The material is decorated with vine plants and ears of corn—symbolizing the bread and wine of the eucharist—and allows the Child's head, crowned as sumptuously as his mother's, to appear at waist height.

Notre-Dame-de-Confession, the famous black Virgin of the crypts of Saint-Victor at Marseilles, offers us a fine specimen of ancient statuary, large and lithe. This figure, full of nobility, holds a sceptre in her right hand and has her forehead encircled with a triple-flowered crown.

Notre Dame of Rocamadour, which by 1166 was already the site of a famous pilgrimage, is a miraculous madonna, the origin of which is attributed to the Jew Zacchaeus, head of the publicans of Jericho. This statue dominates the altar of the Virgin chapel, built in 1479. It is a wooden statuette, blackened by time, wrapped in a robe of silver scales, the worm-eaten remains of which are still preserved. 'The celebrity of Rocamadour goes back to the legendary hermit, St. Amateur or Amadour, who carved a wooden statuette of the Virgin, to which numerous miracles were attributed. It is said that Amateur was the pseudonym of the publican Zacchaeus, who had been converted by Jesus Christ. When Zacchaeus came to Gaul, he propagated the cult of the Virgin. The one at Rocamadour is very ancient, but the great vogue of the pilgrimage dates only from the twelfth century.'[29]

At Vichy, veneration of the black Virgin dates back to 'all antiquity', as the parish priest, Antoine Gravier, reported in the seventeenth century. Archaeologists give this sculpture a fourteenth century dating and, since the oldest parts of the church of St. Blaise, where it stands, were not built until the fifteenth century, Abbé

[29] La grande Encyclopédie, bk. XVIII, p. 761.

Allot, who describes this statue, thinks it was formerly to be found in the St. Nicholas Chapel, founded in 1372 by Guillaume de Hames.

The church of Guéodet at Quimper, still called Notre-Dame-de-la-Cité, also possesses a black Virgin.

Camille Flammarion[30] tells us of a similar statue, which he saw in the vaults of the Observatory on September 24, 1871—two centuries after the first thermometric observation was made there. 'The terrace and balustrade of this collossal Louis XIV edifice,' he writes, 'rise 28 metres above ground level and its foundations go down the same distance—28 metres. At the corner of one of the subterranean galleries, a statuette of the Virgin may be seen, which was placed there in the same year, 1671. Verses engraved at her feet invoke her by the name of *Our Lady Underground*.' This little-known Virgin of Paris, who personifies in the capital the mysterious *subject* of Hermes, appears to be a replica of the one at Chartres, the *Blessed Lady Underground*.

Another detail useful to the hermeticist is that in the ceremonial prescribed for the processions of the black Virgins only *green-coloured* candles were burnt.

As for the statuettes of Isis—I am speaking of those which escaped being Christianized—these are even rarer than the black Virgins. Perhaps one should seek the reason for this in the high antiquity of these icons. Witkowski[31] describes one, which was housed in the St. Etienne Cathedral at Metz. 'This stone figure of Isis,' writes the author, '43 cm. high and 29 cm. broad, came from the old cloister. The high relief projected 18 cm. It represented the naked bust of a woman, but was so thin that, to make use of a picturesque phrase of Abbé Brantôme, "She could not show anything but the outline". Her head was *covered with a veil*. Two dried-up breasts hung down from her chest, like those of the Dianas of Ephesus. The skin was coloured *red* and the drapery covering the figure was *black*. Similar statues were to be found at St. Germain-des-Prés and St. Etienne in Lyons.'

At any rate, what remains for us is the fact that the cult of Isis,

[30] Camille Flammarion. *L'Atmosphère*. Paris, Hachette, 1888, p. 362.
[31] Cf. *L'Art profane à l'Eglise*. Etranger. op. cit., p. 26.

the Egyptian Ceres, was very mysterious. We only know that the feast of the goddess was solemnly celebrated every year at Busiris and that a bull was sacrificed to her. Herodotus says: 'Tens of thousands of men and women, when the sacrifice is over, beat their breasts: in whose honour, however, I do not feel it proper for me to say.' The Greeks, as well as the Egyptians, preserved absolute silence on the mysteries of the cult of Ceres and the historians have not told us anything, which could satisfy our curiosity. *The revelation to the profane of the secret of these practices was punishable by death.* It was even considered a crime to lend an ear to its divulgence. Entry to the temple of Ceres, following the example of the Egyptian sanctuaries of Isis, was regularly forbidden to all those, who had not received initiation. However, the information transmitted to us about the hierarchy of the great priests allows us to conclude that the mysteries of Ceres must have been of the same order as those of the hermetic science. Indeed, we know that the ministers of the cult were divided into four degrees: *the hierophant,* whose task was to instruct the neophytes; *the torch-bearer,* who represented *the sun; the herald,* who represented *Mercury; the minister of the altar,* who represented *the moon.* In Rome, the *Cerealia* were celebrated on April 12 and lasted for a week. In the processions an *egg* was carried, the symbol of the world, and pigs were sacrificed.

I have already mentioned that a stone at Die, representing Isis, referred to her as the *mother of the Gods.* The same epithet was applied to Rhea or Cybele. The two goddesses are thus shown as being nearly related and I would tend to consider them merely as different expressions of one and the same principle. M. Charles Vincens confirms this opinion in the description he gives of a bas-relief featuring Cybele, seen for centuries on the outside of the parochial church of Pennes (Bouches-du-Rhone), with its inscription: *Matri Deum.* 'This curious piece,' he tells us, 'disappeared only around 1610, but it is engraved in Grosson's *Recueil* (p. 20).' It is a curious hermetic analogy that Cybele was worshipped at Pessinonte in Phrygia in the form of a *black stone,* which was said to have *fallen* from heaven. Phidias represents the goddess seated on a throne between *two lions,* having on her head a mural crown, from which hangs a *veil*. Sometimes she is represented holding a *key* and seeming *to draw back her veil*. Isis, Ceres and Cybele are three heads under the same veil.

9

Having disposed of these preliminaries, we must now undertake a hermetic study of the cathedral and, in order to limit our investigations, I will take, as a type, the Christian temple of the French capital, Notre Dame of Paris.

My task is certainly a difficult one. We no longer live in the times of Messire Bernard, Count of Trévise, of Zachaire or of Flamel. The centuries have left their deep mark on the face of the building, the elements have dug broad wrinkles, but the ravages of time count for little in comparison with those wrought by human madness. Revolutions have made their imprint there, a regrettable witness to the anger of the common people. Vandalism, that enemy of beauty, has vented its hatred in terrible mutilations and the restorers themselves, although having the best intentions, have not always known how to respect what the iconoclasts had spared.

The majestic Notre Dame of Paris was formerly raised up on a flight of eleven steps. Separated only by a narrow space from the wooden houses, from the pointed, crow's step gables, it gained in boldness and elegance what it lost in bulk. Today, thanks to clearances, it appears all the more massive for being more isolated and because its porches, pillars and buttresses rest directly on the ground. A gradual raising of the ground level all around has meant that the cathedral steps have been swallowed up, one by one, until none remains.

The space in front of the cathedral was once bordered on one side by the imposing basilica itself and on the other by a picturesque conglomeration of little buildings, decorated with spires, spikes and weathercocks. These were interspersed with painted shops, having carved beams and comic signs. At the corners of the buildings were niches, ornamented with madonnas or saints, flanked with turrets, pepper-pot towers and bastions. In the middle of this space stood a tall, narrow stone statue, holding a book in one hand and a snake in the other. This statue was part of a monumental fountain, on which was written this couplet:

Qui sitis, huc tendas: desunt si forte liquores,
Pergredere, aeternas diva paravit aquas.
You, who are thirsty, come hither: if, by chance the fountain fails
The goddess has, by degrees, prepared the everlasting waters.

The people used to call it sometimes Monsieur Legris (Mr. Grey), sometimes the *Dealer in Grey*, the *Great Fasting Man* or the *Fasting Man of Notre Dame*.

Many interpretations have been given of these strange expressions applied by the common people to an image, which the archaeologists have not been able to identify. The best explanation is the one given by *Amédée of Ponthieu*,[32] which seems to me all the more interesting since the author, who was not a hermeticist, judges without prejudice and without any preconceived idea.

'In front of this temple,' he tells us, 'stood a sacred monolith, which time had rendered shapeless. The ancients called it Phoebigenus,[33] the son of Apollo. Later the people called it *Maître Pierre*, meaning *master stone, stone* of power.[34] It was also called *Messire Legris* (Mr. Grey), since *grey* signified *fire* and particularly *feu grisou* (fire damp), will-o'-the-wisp. . . .

'According to some, these unformed features resemble Esculapius, Mercury, or the god Terminus.[35] According to others they were the features of Archambaud, Mayor of the Palace under Clovis II, who had donated the ground on which the Hotel-Dieu was built. Others saw the features of Guillaume de Paris, who had built it at the same time as the portal of Notre Dame. The Abbé Leboeuf saw the face of Christ; others St. Geneviève, patron saint of Paris.

[32] Amédée de Ponthieu, *Légendes du Vieux Paris*. Paris, Bachelin-Desflorenne, 1867, p. 91.
[33] Engendered by the sun or by gold.
[34] It is the headstone, which I have already mentioned.
[35] The busts of Terminus were busts of Hermes (Mercury).

'This stone was removed in 1748, when the square of the Parvis-de-Notre-Dame was enlarged.'

At about the same time, the chapter of Notre Dame received the order to suppress the statue of St. Christopher. This collossus, painted in grey, stood back to the first pillar on the right, as you enter the nave. It had been erected in 1413 by Antoine des Essarts, Chamberlain to King Charles VI. Its removal was suggested in 1772, but Christopher de Beaumont, Archbishop of Paris at that time, opposed this formally. It was only at his death in 1781 that it was dragged away and broken up. Notre Dame of Amiens still has a good Christian giant carrying the Child Jesus, but it must have escaped destruction only because it forms part of a wall. It is a sculpture in bas-relief. Seville Cathedral has also preserved a collossal St. Christopher, in the form of a fresco. The St. Christopher in the church of St. Jacques-la-Boucherie was destroyed, with the building, and Auxerre Cathedral's fine statue, dating from 1539, was destroyed by order in 1768, only a few years before the one in Paris.

Behind such acts there must obviously have been powerful motives. Although they do not appear to me to be justified, we can, however, find their cause in the symbolical expression drawn from the legend condensed—doubtless all too clearly—by the image. St. Christopher, whose primitive name *Offerus*, is revealed to us by Jacques de Voragine, signifies to the masses: *he, who carries Christ* (from the Greek Χρίστοφόρος); but the phonetic cabala discloses another meaning, which is adequate and in conformity with the hermetic doctrine. Christopher stands for Chrysopher: *he, who carries gold* (Greek Χρυσοφόρος). From this one can better understand the extreme importance of the symbol of St. Christopher. It is the hieroglyph of the *solar sulphur* (Jesus), of the *nascent gold*, raised on the mercurial waters and then carried, by the proper energy of this Mercury, to the degree of power possessed by the Elixir. According to Aristotle, the emblematic colour of Mercury is *grey* or *violet*, which explains sufficiently why the statutes of St. Christopher were given a coating of that colour. A certain number of old engravings of the collossus, kept at the Cabinet des Estampes in the Bibliothèque Nationale, are executed in simple outline in *bistre*. The oldest dates from 1418.

At Rocamadour (Lot), they still point out a gigantic statue of St. Christopher, raised up on the St. Michael heights and pre-dating the church. Beside it an old *iron-bound chest* is to be seen, above which the rough stump of a sword is sticking out of the rock and secured with a chain. Legend would have it that this fragment was part of the famous sword Durandal, which the paladin Roland broke, when making the breach at Roncevaux. However that may be, the truth behind these symbols is highly transparent. The sword, which opens up the rock, Moses' rod, which made water flow from the rock of Horeb, the sceptre of the goddess Rhea, with which she struck the Mount Dyndimus and the javelin of Atalanta are all one and the same hieroglyph of this hidden matter of the Philosophers, whose nature is indicated by St. Christopher and the result by the iron-bound chest.

I am sorry not to be able to say more about this magnificent emblem, which had the first place reserved for it in the gothic basilicas. No precise and detailed description has come down to us of those great figures, those groups, which were admirable in their teaching, but which a superficial and decadent age removed, without even the excuse of urgent necessity.

The eighteenth century, the reign of the aristocracy and of wit, of courtly priests, powdered marquises, bewigged gentlemen; that age, blessed with dancing-masters, madrigals and Watteau shepherdesses; that brilliant and perverse, frivolous and mannered century, which was to be submerged in blood, was particularly hostile to gothic works of art. Carried along by the great tide of decadence, which, under Francis I, took the paradoxical name of the Renaissance, the artists of the time were incapable of making an effort equal to that of their ancestors. Being entirely ignorant of medieval symbolism, they applied themselves to reproducing bastard works without taste, without character, without esoteric thought, rather than to pursuing and developing admirable and healthy French originality.

Architects, painters and sculptors, preferring their own glory to that of the Art, looked to ancient models, copied in Italy.

The builders of the Middle Ages had the natural attributes of faith and modesty. The anonymous creators of pure works of art,

E

they built for Truth, for the affirmation of their ideal, for the propagation and the nobility of their science. Those of the Renaissance, preoccupied above all by their personality, jealous of their worth, built for their own future fame. The Middle Ages owed their splendour to the originality of their creations; the Renaissance owed its vogue to the servile fidelity of its copies. The former was an idea; the latter, a fashion. On one side, genius; on the other, talent. In gothic art, the actual execution remains subordinate to the idea; in Renaissance art, it dominates and obliterates the idea. The one appeals to the heart, to the brain, to the soul; it is the triumph of spirit. The other is directed to the senses; it is the glorification of matter. From the twelfth to the fifteenth century, there was poverty of media, but a wealth of expression; from the sixteenth century onwards, art has shown beauty of form, but mediocrity of invention. The medieval masters knew how to animate common limestone; the artists of the Renaissance left their marble inert and cold.

It is the antagonism of these two periods, born of opposing concepts, which explains the scorn, shown by the Renaissance, and its deep hatred of everything gothic.

Such a state of mind was bound to be fatal to the work of the Middle Ages; and it is, indeed, to this that we must attribute the innumerable mutilations, which we deplore today.

Paris

1

The Cathedral of Paris, like most French cathedrals, is dedicated to the Blessed Virgin Mary or the Virgin Mother. The common people of France call these churches *Notre-Dames*. In Sicily, they have the even more expressive name of the *Matrices*. Thus there are many temples dedicated to the *Mother* (Lat. *mater*, *matris*), to the *Matrona* in the primitive sense, a word which has been corrupted into *Madonna* (Ital. *ma donna*), my Lady, and, by extension, Our Lady (*Notre-Dame*).

Let us pass the railing of the porch and begin our study of the façade with the great portal, called the Central Porch, or Porch of Judgment.

The pier, which divides the entrance bay, shows a series of allegorical representations of the medieval sciences. In the place of honour, facing the parvis, alchemy is represented by a woman, with her head touching the clouds. Seated on a throne, she holds in her left hand a sceptre, the sign of royal power, while her right hand supports two books, one closed (esotericism), the other open (exotericism). Supported between her knees and leaning against her chest, is the ladder with nine rungs—*scala philosophorum*—hieroglyph of the patience which the faithful must possess in the course of the nine successive operations of the hermetic labour (plate II). 'Patience is the Philosophers' ladder,' Valois[1] tells us, 'and humility is the door to their garden; for whosoever will persevere without pride and without envy, on him God will show mercy.'

That is the title of the philosophical chapter of this *Mutus Liber*, the gothic cathedral; the frontispiece of this occult Bible, with its massive pages of stone; the imprint, the seal of the secular Great Work on the very face of the Christian Great Work. It could not be better situated than on the very threshold of the main entrance. Thus the cathedral appears to be based on alchemical science, on the science which investigates the transformations of the original substance, elementary matter (Lat. *materea*, root *mater* mother). For the Virgin Mother, stripped of her symbolical veil, is none other than the personification of the primitive substance, used by the Principle, the creator of all that is, for the furtherance of his designs. This is the meaning (and, indeed, a very clear one) of this strange epithet, which we read in the Mass of the Immaculate Conception of the Virgin, of which the text reads:

'The Lord possessed me at the beginning of his ways. I existed before he formed any creature. I existed from all eternity, before the earth was created. The abysses were not yet and already I was conceived. The fountains had not yet come out of the earth; the heavy mass of the mountains had not yet been formed; I was begotten before the hills. He had created neither the earth, nor the rivers, nor strengthened the world on its poles. When he prepared the heavens, I was present; when he confined the abysses within

[1] *Oeuvres de Nicolas Grosparmy et Nicolas Valois*. Mss. Biblioth. de L'Arsenal, no. 2516 (166 S.A.F.), p. 176.

II. ALCHEMY
Bas-relief on the Great Porch of Notre-Dame, Paris.

their bounds and prescribed an inviolable law; when he confirmed the air above the earth; when he balanced the waters of the fountains; when he shut up the sea within its limits and imposed a law on the waters, so that they should not pass their bounds; when he laid the foundations of the earth, *I was with him* and I regulated all things.'

Obviously what is dealt with here is the *very essence of things.* Indeed, the Litanies tell us that the Virgin is the *Vase containing the Spirit of things: vas spirituale.* 'On a table, breast high to the Magi,' Etteila[2] tells us, 'were on one side a book or a series of golden pages or plates (the book of Thoth) and on the other side a *vase full of* celestial-astral *liquid,* consisting of one part of wild honey, one part of terrestial water and a third part of celestial water. . . . The secret, the mystery was therefore in this vase.'

This singular virgin—virgo singularis as the Church expressly calls her—is, in addition, glorified under names which denote clearly enough her positive origin. Is she not also called the Palm tree of Patience (*Palma patientiae*) the Lily among the thorns.[3] (*Lilium inter spinas*); Sampson's *symbolic Honey*; *Gideon's Fleece*; the *mystic Rose*; the *Gateway to Heaven*; the *House of Gold*, etc. The same texts also call Mary the *Seat of Wisdom*, in other words the *subject of the* hermetic *science* of universal wisdom. In the symbolism of planetary metals, she is the *Moon*, who receives the rays of the Sun and keeps them secretly in her breast. She is the dispenser of the passive substance, which the solar spirit comes to animate. Mary, Virgin and Mother, then, represents form; Elias, the Sun, God the Father, is the emblem of the vital spirit. From the union of these two principles living matter results, subject to the vicissitudes of the laws of mutation and progression. Thus is *Jesus*, the incarnate spirit, fire, incorporated in things here below:

AND THE WORD WAS MADE FLESH, AND DWELT AMONG US

On the other hand, the Bible tells us that Mary, mother of Jesus, was of the stem of *Jesse.* Now, the Hebrew word *Jes* means *fire,*

[2] Etteila, *Le Denier du Pauvre*, in the *Sept nuances de l'oeuvre philosophique*, (1786). p. 57.

[3] This is the title of the famous alchemical manuscripts of Agricola and Ticinensis. Cf. libraries of Rennes (159); of Bordeaux (533); of Lyons (154); of Cambrai (919).

the *Sun Divinity*. To be of the stem of Jesse is thus to be of the race of the sun, of fire. Since matter derives from the solar *fire*, as we have just seen, the very name of *Jesus* appears to us in its original and celestial splendour: *fire, sun, God*.

Finally, in the *Ave Regina*, the Virgin is properly called *root* (*salve radix*) to show that she is the principle and the beginning of all things. 'Hail, root by which the Light has shone on the world.'

These are the reflections suggested by the expressive bas-relief, which greets the visitor under the porch of the basilica. Hermetic philosophy, the ancient spagyric art, welcomes him to the gothic church, the alchemical temple *par excellence*. For the whole cathedral is just a silent witness in images to the ancient science of Hermes, and it has even managed to preserve one of its ancient craftsmen. Notre Dame has indeed kept its alchemist.

If, moved by curiosity or simply wishing to give some purpose to a summer stroll, you climb the spiral staircase leading to the high parts of the building, you should make you way slowly along the path, hollowed out like a channel at the top of the second gallery. Once you are in the vicinity of the main axis of the majestic building, at the re-entrant angle of the North Tower, you will see in the middle of the procession of monsters, a large and striking stone relief of an old man. This is he—the alchemist of Notre Dame (pl. III).

Wearing a Phrygian cap, attribute of the Adept,[4] negligently placed on his long, thickly curling hair, the scholar, dressed in his

---

[4] The Phrygian cap, which was worn by the sans-culottes and acted as a sort of protective talisman in the midst of the revolutionary slaughter, was a distinctive sign of the Initiates. In the analysis, which he made of a work of Lombard (de Langres) entitled *Histoire des Jacobins, depuis 1789 jusqu'à ce jour, ou Etat de l'Europe en novembre 1820* (Paris 1820), the scholar Pierre Dujols writes that for the grade of the Epopt (in the Eleusinian Mysteries) the new member was asked whether he felt in himself the strength, the will and the devotion necessary for him to set his hand to the GREAT WORK. Then a red cap was put on his head, while this formula was pronounced: 'Cover yourself with this cap, it is worth more than a king's crown.' Few suspected that this hat, called *liberia* in the *Mithraic rituals* and which formerly denoted the freed slaves, was a masonic symbol and the supreme mark of Initiation. It is not therefore surprising to see it represented on our coins and our public monuments.

III. NOTRE-DAME, PARIS
The Alchemist.

working cape, is leaning with one hand on the balustrade and stroking his full, silky beard with the other. He is not meditating, he is observing. His eye is fixed; his look is strangely acute. The philosopher's whole attitude suggests extreme emotion. The slope of his shoulders, the forward thrust of his head and chest, betray, indeed, the greatest surprise. Surely that hand of stone is coming to life. Is it illusion? You would think you saw it trembling. . . .

What a splendid figure he is, this old master! Anxiously and attentively he is scrutinizing and enquiring into the evolution of mineral life and finally he contemplates in amazement the prodigy, which his faith alone has let him perceive. And how poor are the modern statues of our learned men—whether thew are cast in bronze or sculpted in marble—set beside this venerable figure, so simple, yet so powerfully realistic.

2

The basement of the façade, which extends below the three porches, is entirely dedicated to our science, and this collection of images, as strange as they are instructive, is a veritable feast for anyone who deciphers hermetic enigmas.

It is here that we are going to find in stone the name of the *subject of the Wise*; here that we shall witness the processing of the secret solvent, and here, finally, that we shall follow, step by step, the work of making the Elixir, from calcination to ultimate coction.

But, in order to keep some sort of method in this study, we shall always observe the order in which the figures succeed one another, proceeding from the exterior to the door of the porch, as the faithful would do on entering the sanctuary. On the lateral surfaces of the piers on each side of the great doorway, we shall find two little bas-reliefs at eye level, each fitting into a pointed arch. The one on the left pillar shows us the alchemist discovering the *mysterious Fountain*, which Le Trévisan describes in the last *Parable* of his book on *la Philosophie naturelle des Métaux.*[5]

[5] Cf. J. Mangin de Richebourg, *Bibliothèque des Philosophes Chimiques.* Paris, 1741, bk. II, treatise VII.

The artist has come a long way; he has taken false turnings and wandered on doubtful paths; but finally his joy bursts forth! The stream of *living water* flows at his feet; it gushes out bubbling from the *old hollow oak*.[6] Our adept has hit the target. And so, scorning the bow and arrows with which, like Cadmus, he pierced the serpent, he watches the welling of this clear spring, whose virtue as a solvent and whose volatile spirit are indicated to him by a bird, perched on the tree (pl. IV).

But what is this occult *Fountain*? What is the nature of this powerful solvent, capable of penetrating every metal—gold in particular—and, with the help of the dissolved body, of accomplishing the great task in its entirety? These are such deep riddles, that they have discouraged a considerable number of seekers. All, or almost all, have battered their heads against the impenetrable wall set up by the Philosophers to guard their citadel.

In mythology it is called *Libethra*[7] and is said to have been a fountain of *Magnesia*. Near it was another spring, called the *Rock*. Both of them *issued from a large rock*, shaped like a woman's bosom, the water seeming to *flow like milk from her two breasts*. Now, we know that the ancient authors called the matter of the work *our Magnesia* and that the liquid extracted from this magnesia is called *Virgin's Milk*. Here, there is a clue. As for the allegory of the mixing or combination of this primitive water, issuing from the Chaos of the Wise, with a second water, different in nature (although of the same kind), this allegory is clear enough and sufficiently expressive. This combination gives rise to a third *water which does not wet the hands*, which the Philosophers have sometimes called *Mercury*, sometimes *Sulphur*, according to whether they were considering the *quality* of this water or its physical *aspect*.

In the treatise on the Azoth,[8] attributed to that famous monk of Erfurth, Basil Valentine, but which seems rather to have been the

---

[6] Flamel says simply 'Note this oak' in the *Livre des Figures hiéroglyphiques*.

[7] Cf. Noel, *Dictionnaire de la Fable*. Paris, le Normant, 1801.

[8] *Azoth* or *Moyen de faire l'Or caché des Philosophes* by Basil Valentine. Paris, Pierre Moet, 1659, p. 51.

IV.   NOTRE-DAME, PARIS
The mysterious Fountain at the foot of the Old Oak.

work of Senior Zadith, there is a woodcut representing a crowned nymph or siren, swimming in the sea and making two jets of milk spurt from her rounded breasts to mingle with the waves.

The Arab authors called this Fountain *Holmat*. They tell us further that its waters bestowed immortality on the prophet Elias (Ηλίος, the sun). They located this famous spring in the *Modhallam*, a word whose root means *dark and gloomy sea*, which brings out clearly the elemental confusion which the Wise attributed to their *Chaos* or first matter.

There was a painted version of the fable I have just mentioned in the little church of Brixen (Tyrol). This strange picture, described by Misson and mentioned by Witkowski,[9] appears to be a religious version of the same chemical theme. 'Jesus makes the blood from his side, pierced by the lance of Longinus, flow into a large bowl; the Virgin squeezes her breasts and the milk spurting from them falls into the same receptacle. The overflow goes into a second bowl and is lost down an abyss of flame. There, souls in Purgatory—of both sexes and with breasts bared—make haste to receive this precious liquid, which comforts and refreshes them.'

At the bottom of this old painting is an inscription in Church Latin:

> *Dum fluit e Christi benedicto Vulnere sanguis,*
> *Et dum Virgineum lac pia Virgo premit,*
> *Lac fuit et sanguis, sanguis conjungitur et lac,*
> *Et sit Fons Vitae, Fons et Origo boni.*[10]

It is said that the Adept, Nicholas Flamel, possessed a book[11] giving the *Symbolical Figures of Abraham the Jew*, which he displayed in his scribe's booth. Among the descriptions accompanying these figures, I would mention two, which refer to the *mysterious*

[9] G. J. Witkowski, *L'Art profane a l'Eglise*. Etranger, p. 63.

[10] While the blood flows from the blessed wound of Christ and the holy Virgin presses her virginal breast, the milk and the blood spurt out and are mixed and become the Fountain of Life and the Spring of Well-being.

[11] *Recueil de Sept Figures peintes*. Bibl. de l'Arsenal, no. 3047 (153 S.A.F.).

Fountain and its components. Here is the original text of these two captions:

'The third figure depicts and represents a garden enclosed by a hedge and having many beds. In the middle there is an *old, hollow oak,* at the foot of which, on one side, there is a rose tree with *golden leaves* and *white and red roses.* This rose tree encompasses the oak all the way up, close to its branches. *At the foot of this hollow oak there bubbles a fountain,* as clear as silver, which disappears into the ground. Among those who seek it are four blind men, who are hoeing for it, and four others, who are looking for it without digging. The *fountain is in front of them,* but they cannot find it, except one man, who weighs the water in his hand.'

It is this last character, who is the subject of the sculptured motif at Notre Dame of Paris. The preparation of the solvent in question is related in the explanation, which accompanies the next figure:

'Fourth figure. A field is depicted in which a *crowned king, dressed in red* in the Jewish fashion, holds a naked sword. Two soldiers are killing the children of two mothers, while the mothers, sitting on the ground, weep for their little ones. Two other soldiers pour blood into a large bowl, full of the said blood, while the *sun and moon* descend from the sky or the clouds *to bathe* in it. There are six soldiers clad in white armour, the king making the seventh, and there are also *seven* dead *innocents* and *two mothers,* one of whom, weeping and wiping her face with a handkerchief, is *dressed in blue,* while the other, also weeping, is *dressed in red.'*

Let me also mention a figure in Trismosin's book,[12] which is more or less similar to Abraham's third figure. It shows an oak, from whose foot—encircled by a gold crown—issues a secret stream, which flows away into the distance. In the foliage of the tree, white birds are disporting themselves, with the exception of a crow, which appears to be asleep and which a poorly-dressed man on a ladder is about to catch. In the foreground of this rustic scene there are two sophists, elegantly dressed in sumptuous materials, who are discussing and arguing a scientific point, without noticing the oak tree behind and without seeing the Fountain flowing at their feet. . . .

[12] Cf. Trismosin, *La Toyson d'Or.* Paris, Ch. Sevestre, 1612, p. 52.

Finally, let me add that the esoteric tradition of the *Fountain of Life* or the *Fountain of Youth* may be found in material form in the *sacred Wells* associated with most gothic churches in the Middle Ages. The water drawn from them was usually thought to have curative value and was used in the treatment of certain illnesses. Abbon, in his poem on the Siege of Paris by the Normans, reports various incidents attesting to the marvellous properties of the water from the well of St. Germain-des-Près, which was bored at the back of the sanctuary of the celebrated abbey church. Similarly, the water from the well of St. Marcellus in Paris, dug in the church near the tombstone of the venerable bishop, was found, according to Gregory of Tours, to be a powerful remedy for various diseases. To this day there exists a miraculous holy well, called the Well of the Holy Virgin, inside the gothic church of Notre Dame at Lepine (Marne) and a similar well in the middle of the choir of Notre Dame at Limoux (Aude), whose water is said to cure all diseases. It bears this inscription:

Omnis qui bibit hanc aquam, si fidem addit, salvus erit.

Whoever drinks this water will be cured, provided he also believes.

I shall soon have occasion to refer again to this *pontic water*, to which the Philosophers have given a host of more or less suggestive names.

On the opposite pier, facing the carved motif explaining the properties and the nature of the secret agent, we can watch the coction of the philosophic *compost*. This time, the artist watches over the product of his labour. Our knight, clad in armour, with greaves on his legs and his shield on his arm, has taken up his position on what seems to be the rampart of a fortress, judging by the battlements which surround it. With a defensive movement he holds his javelin against some indistinct form (rays? tongues of flame?), which it is unfortunately impossible to identify because the moulding is so mutilated. Behind the warrior, a strange little building, composed of a crenellated, arched base supported on four pillars, is crowned by a segmented dome with a spherical keystone.

A pointed and flaming mass under the lower archway shows clearly the use to which this is to be put. This curious tower, a miniature castle, is the instrument of the Great Work, the *Athenor*, the occult furnace with two flames—potential and actual—known to all disciples, but debased by the great number of descriptions and pictures made of it (pl. V).

Immediately above these figures are reproduced two subjects, which seem to form a complement to them, but, since the esoteric meaning is here hidden behind sacred subjects and scenes from the Bible, I shall avoid speaking about them, to evade reproach for an arbitrary interpretation. Some great scholars among the ancient masters have not been afraid to explain the parables of scripture in alchemical terms, since they may be interpreted in so many ways. Hermetic Philosophy often invokes the authority of Genesis as an analogy to the first task of the Work. A number of allegories from the Old and New Testament take on an unexpected aspect when related to alchemy. Such precedents should both encourage me and present me with an excuse. However, I prefer to use only those themes which are of an indisputably profane nature, leaving gentle investigators to draw their own conclusions about the others.

3

The hermetic subjects on the stylobate extend in two rows, one above the other, to the right and left of the porch. The lower row is composed of twelve medallions and the upper of twelve figures. The latter represent personages seated on solid pedestals with grooved ornament, sometimes recessed and sometimes in relief, placed between the pillars of trilobate arcades. All the figures hold discs ornamented with various emblems, relating to the alchemical work.

Beginning with the upper row, left hand side, the first bas-relief shows the image of the crow, symbol of the *colour black*. The woman, who holds it on her lap, symbolizes *Putrefaction*.

V.   NOTRE-DAME, PARIS—PORCH OF JUDGMENT
The Alchemist protects the Athenor against external influences.

VI.   NOTRE-DAME, PARIS—CENTRAL PORCH
The Crow—Putrefaction.

Let us pause a moment at the hieroglyph of the *Crow*, because it conceals an important point of our science. In fact, in the coction of the philosophical Rebis, it represents the *colour black* or the first appearance of decomposition, resulting from the perfect mixture of the matters of the *Egg*. According to the Philosophers, that is a certain indication of future success; the outward sign of the exact preparation of the compost. The *Crow* is, in a sense, the official seal of the Work, in the same way that the star is the signature of the initial subject.

However, this blackness which the Artist hopes to obtain, which he anxiously awaits, the sight of which satisfies his desires and fills him with joy, does not appear only during the coction. The black bird shows itself several times and this frequency makes it possible for the authors to introduce confusion into the order of the operations.

According to Le Breton,[13] 'There are *four putrefactions* in the philosophic work. The first is the first separation; the second in the first conjunction; the third in the second conjunction of the heavy water with its salt; finally, the fourth in the fixation of the sulphur. In each one of these putrefactions, the blackness comes.'

So our old masters have had sport in covering the secret with a heavy veil, in mixing the specific qualities of the various substances during the four operations which show the black colour. Thus it becomes very laborious to separate them and to define clearly what belongs to each one of them.

Here are some quotations, which may enlighten the investigator and enable him to find his way through this murky labyrinth.

'In the second operation,' writes Le Chevalier Inconnu,[14] 'the wise artist fixes the general soul of the world in common gold and purifies the earthly and immobile soul. In this operation the putrefaction, which they call the *Crow's Head*, is very long. This is followed by a third multiplication, by adding the philosophic matter or the general soul of the world.'

Two successive operations are clearly indicated here, the first of

[13] Le Breton, *Clefs de la Philosophie Spagyrique.* Paris, Jombert, 1722, p. 282.
[14] *La Nature à découvert*, by Le Chevalier Inconnu. Aix, 1669.

which ends and the second begins after the appearance of the black coloration—which is not the case in coction.

A valuable anonymous manuscript of the eighteenth century[15] speaks as follows of this first putrefaction, which must not be confused with the others:

'If the matter is not corrupted and mortified,' says this work, 'you cannot extract our elements and our principles; and, in order to help you in this difficulty, I will give you signs by which to recognize it. Some Philosophers have also pointed this out. Morien says: "It must show some acidity and have a certain *smell of the grave*." Philalethes says that it must appear like *fish's eyes*, that is to say little bubbles on the surface, and it must appear to foam; for that is a sign that the matter is fermenting and boiling. This fermentation is extremely lengthy and you must have plenty of patience, because it is done by our *secret fire*, which is the only agent capable of opening, subliming and putrefying.'

But, of all the descriptions, those referring to the *crow* (or black colour) of the coction are by far the most numerous and the most fundamental, because they embrace the character of all the other operations.

Bernard Trévisan expresses himself thus:

'Note that when our compost begins to be steeped in our permanent water, then all the compost becomes like melted pitch and is all blackened like coal. And at this point our compost is called: *black pitch, burnt salt, molten lead, impure latten, Magnesia* and *John's Blackbird*. For now a *black cloud* is seen, floating sweetly and gently through the middle part of the vessel and being raised above the vessel; and at the bottom of the latter is the matter, melted like pitch, and remaining totally dissolved. Jacques du Bourg St. Saturnin speaks of this cloud, saying: "Oh blessed cloud which floats through our vessel!" This is the eclipse of the sun, of which Raymond[16] speaks. And when this mass is thus blackened, it is said to be dead and deprived of its form. . . . The humidity is shown coloured like quick-silver, black and stinking. Formerly it was dry, white, sweet-smelling and ardent, freed from sulphur in the first

---

[15] *La Clef du Cabinet hermétique.* Eighteenth century Mss. Anon.
[16] The author means Raymond Lully (Doctor Illuminatus).

operation and now to be purified by this second operation. And, therefore, this body is deprived of its soul, which it has lost, and of the splendour and marvellous clearness, which it had at first, and is now black and ugly. . . . This mass, which is black or blackened in this way, is the key,[17] the beginning and the sign of the discovery of the perfect way of working the second process of our precious stone. "For this reason," says Hermes, "when the blackness is seen, have faith that you have been on the right path and have kept to the right way".'

Batsdorff, presumed by some to be the author of a classic work,[18] which others attribute to Gaston de Claves, teaches that the putrefaction begins when the blackness appears and that it is then the sign of a task performed exactly and in accordance with nature. He adds: 'The Philosophers have given it various names, such as *the West*, the *Shadows*, the *Eclipse, Leprosy*, the *Crow's Head, Death*, the *Mortification of Mercury*. . . . It appears, then, that through this putrefaction a separation is made of the pure and the impure. Further, the signs of a good and true putrefaction are a very intense or deep blackness and a foul and offensive *smell*, called *toxicum et venenum* by the Philosophers, a smell, however, which cannot be perceived by the nose but only by the understanding.'

It would not be of any further use to the student to continue with these quotations, so let us stop them now and return to the hermetic figures of Notre Dame.

The second Bas-relief shows us the effigy of philosophic Mercury: a snake coiled round a golden wand. Abraham the Jew, also known as Eleazor, made use of it in the book which came into the possession of Flamel—which is in no way surprising, since we meet with this symbol during the whole medieval period (pl. VII).

The snake indicates the incisive and solvent nature of the Mercury, which avidly absorbs the metallic sulphur and holds it so powerfully that the cohesion cannot later be overcome. This is the 'poisoned worm, which infects everything with its venom', men-

---

[17] The name *key* is given to every radical (i.e. irreducible) alchemical solution and this term is sometimes extended to the Menstrua or solvents which can bring it about.

[18] *Le Filet d'Ariadne*. Paris, d'Houry, 1695, p. 99.

F

tioned in *L'Ancienne Guerre des Chevaliers*.[19] This reptile is the aspect of *Mercury in its first state* and the golden wand is the corporeal sulphur, which is added to it. The solution of the sulphur, or, in other words, its absorption by the mercury, has given rise to a great diversity of emblems; but the resulting body, which is homogeneous and perfectly prepared, retains *Philosophers' Mercury* as its name and the caduceus as its symbol. It is the first class matter or *compound*, the *vitriolated egg*, which requires only gradual cooking in order to be transformed first into *red sulphur*, then into *Elixir*, and the third time into the *universal Medicine*. 'In our work,' the Philosophers affirm, 'Mercury alone is sufficient.'

A woman, her long hair streaming like flame, comes next. She personifies *Calcination* and holds against her chest the disc of the *Salamander*, 'which lives in the fire and feeds on fire'. This fabulous lizard stands for nothing else but the incombustible and fixed central salt, which preserves its nature even in the ashes of the calcinated metals and which the ancients called *metallic seed*. The parts of the body which can be burnt are destroyed in the violence of the igneous process; only the pure, unalterable parts resist and, although they are very fixed, they can be extracted by percolation.

This is, at least, the *spagyric* expression of calcination, a simile used by authors to exemplify the general idea which one should have of the hermetic work. However, our masters in the Art have been careful to draw the reader's attention to the fundamental difference which exists between ordinary calcination, such as is carried out in chemical laboratories, and the one which the Initiate operates in the philosopher's closet. The latter kind of calcination is not achieved by any ordinary fire and does not need the assistance of any reflector, but requires the help of an *occult* agent, of a *secret fire*, which, to give a hint about its form, is more like water than flame. This *fire* or *burning water* is the vital spark communicated by the Creator to inert matter, it is the *spirit* enclosed within things,

[19] With the addition of a commentary by Limojon de St. Didier, in the *Triomphe hermétique* or the *Pierre philosophale victorieuse*. Amsterdam, Weitsten, 1699, and Desbordes, 1710.

This rare work has been re-edited by *Atlantis*, and includes the symbolical frontispiece, as well as the explanation of it, which are often omitted in the old copies.

VII.   NOTRE-DAME, PARIS—CENTRAL PORCH
Philosophic Mercury.

VIII.   NOTRE-DAME, PARIS—CENTRAL PORCH
The Salamander—Calcination.

the imperishable *fiery ray* imprisoned at the bottom of the dark, formless and frigid substance. Here I touch on the greatest secret of the Work. Remembering, alas, that I myself was held up by this difficulty for more than twenty years, I would gladly cut this Gordian knot for the benefit of those aspiring to our Science, were I allowed to profane a mystery, whose revelation rests with the *Father of Lights*. To my great regret, I can do no more than point out the danger and, in company with the most eminent philosophers, advise you to read attentively Artephius,[20] Pontanus[21] and the little work, entitled: *Epistola de Igne Philosophorum*.[22] There you will find valuable indications of the nature and characteristics of this *watery fire* or *fiery water*. These teachings can be completed by the two following texts.

The anonymous author of the *Préceptes du Père Abraham* says: 'This *primitive* and celestial *water* must be drawn from the body where it resides, which body, in my opinion, is expressed in seven letters, signifying the cause of all beings, a cause not specifically limited to the house of Aries in engendering its son. It is to this water that the Philosophers have given so many names and it is the universal solvent, the life and health of everything. The Philosophers say that it is in this water that the sun and moon bathe and that they dissolve of their own accord in this water, which is their first origin. It is through this dissolution that they are said to die, but their spirits are carried on the waters of this sea, in which they were swallowed up. . . . Whatever people say, my son, about there being other ways of dissolving these bodies into their first matter, hold fast to what I am telling you, because I know it from experience and from the transmission of the Ancients.'

Limojon de St. Didier writes in the same way: 'The *secret fire* of the Wise is a fire which the Artist prepares according to the Art, or which he can at any rate have prepared by those having perfect knowledge of chemistry. This fire is not really hot, but it is a *fiery spirit* introduced into a subject having the same nature as the Stone; and, being moderately excited by the exterior fire, it calcines

[20] *Le Secret Livre d'Artephius*, in *Trois Traitez de la Philosophie naturelle*. Paris, Marette, 1612.
[21] Pontanus, *De Lapide Philosophico*, Frankfurt, 1614.
[22] Mss. of the Bibliothèque nationale, 1969.

the Stone, dissolves it, sublimes it and *turns it into dry water*, as the Cosmopolite says.'

Further, we shall soon find other figures referring either to the production or to the qualities of this *secret fire enclosed in water*, which constitutes the universal solvent. Now, the matter which is used to prepare it is the very object of the fourth motif: a man shows an image of the *Ram* and holds in his right hand an object, which unfortunately cannot be distinguished today (pl. IX). Is it a mineral, a fragment of an emblem, a utensil, or a piece of material? I do not know. Time and vandalism have had their way. At any rate, the *Ram* remains, and the man, the hieroglyph of the male metallic principle, personifies it. This helps us to understand these words of Pernety: 'The Adepts say that they draw their steel from the belly of Aries, and they also call this *steel* their *lodestone*.'

This is succeeded by *Evolution*, showing the oriflamme, with its three pennants, the triple *colours of the Work*, which are described in all the classical works (pl. X).

The three colours succeed one another in an invariable order, going from *black*, through *white*, to *red*. But since, according to the old saying, *Natura non facit saltus*—nature does not proceed by a leap, there are many intermediate stages between these three principal ones. The artist does not attach much importance to them, because they are superficial and fleeting. They serve only as a witness to the continuity and the progress of the internal changes. As for the main colours, they last longer than these transitory shades and have a profound effect on the matter itself, marking a change of state into chemical constitution. None of those fugitive and more or less brilliant tints are meant here, which play upon the surface of the bath; but rather the colourings within the body itself, which are translated to the outside and which reabsorb all the others. I believe it wise to stress this important point.

These coloured phases, referring specifically to the coction phase in the Great Work, have always served as a symbolical prototype. A precise meaning, and sometimes quite a lengthy one, was attributed to each of them in order that they might be used as a veil, behind which certain concrete truths might be given. In this way a *language of colours*, intimately connected with religion, has been in

IX. NOTRE-DAME, PARIS—CENTRAL PORCH
Preparation of the Universal Solvent.

X.   NOTRE-DAME, PARIS—CENTRAL PORCH
Evolution—colours and processes of the Great Work.

existence at all times. Portal[23] states this and it reappears in the Middle Ages in the stained glass windows of the gothic cathedrals.

The *colour black* was given to Saturn. In spagyric art he is the hieroglyph for *lead*; in astrology, a maleficent planet; in hermeticism, the *black dragon* or *Philosophers' Lead*; in magic, the *black Hen*, etc. In the Egyptian temples, when a new member was about to undergo the initiatory ordeals, a priest approached him and whispered this mysterious sentence in his ear: 'Remember that Osiris is a *black god!*' This is the symbolical colour of the shades and the *Cimmerian darkness*, the colour of Satan, to whom black roses were offered. It is also the colour of primitive *Chaos*, in which the seeds of all things are confused and mixed. It is the *sable* of the science of heraldry and the emblem of the element *earth*, of *night* and *death*.

Just as in Genesis day succeeds night, so light succeeds darkness. Its signature is the colour *White*. The Wise assure us that when their matter has reached this degree, it is freed from all impurity, perfectly cleansed and very exactly purified. It then takes on the appearance of solid granulations or shining corpuscles, reflecting like diamonds and of a dazzling whiteness. White has also been used to denote purity, simplicity and innocence. White is the colour of the Initiates, because the man, who abandons darkness to follow light, passes from the profane state to that of the *Initiate*, the *Pure*. He is spiritually renewed. 'This term white,' says Pierre Dujols, 'has been chosen for very profound psychological reasons. The colour white, as most languages attest, has always denoted *nobility*, *candour* and *purity*. According to the famous *Dictionnaire-Manuel hébreu et chaldéen* of Gesenius, *hur, heur*, signifies *to be white*; *hurim, heurim*, designates the *noble ones*, the *white ones*, the *pure ones*. This more or less variable transcription of Hebrew (*hur, heur, hurim, heurim*) leads us to the French word *heureux* (happy). The *bienheureux* (blessed ones)—those who have been reborn and washed in the blood of the Lamb—are always represented with white garments. Everyone knows that *bienheureux* (the blessed) is also the equivalent, the synonym of the *Initiate*, the *noble one*, the

[23] Frédéric Portal, *Des Couleurs Symboliques*. Paris, Treuttel et Würtz, 1857, p. 2.

pure one. Again, the Initiates wore *white*. The nobles dressed in
the same colour. In Egypt, the shades were similarly dressed in
white. Ptah, the *Regenerator*, was also clad in white, in order to
show the new birth of the *Pure Ones* or the *White Ones*. The
Cathars, a sect to which the *Bianchi* of Florence belonged, were the
Pure Ones (from the Greek Καθαρός). . . . On the other hand,
the Hebrew *schher* represents a transitional black, that is to say the
Ariadne, the *spider* in the middle of its web—the empty *shell*, the
beginning of the funeral Rites," says Portal, "represents that state
of soul which is passing from night to day, from death into life".'

As for *red*, the symbol of fire, it shows exaltation, predominance
of spirit over matter, sovereignty, power and apostleship. The
Philosophic Stone, obtained in the volatile and fusible form of
crystal or red powder, becomes penetrating and capable of curing
leprosy; that is to say of transmuting into gold those ordinary
metals whose tendency to rust renders them inferior, imperfect,
'sick or infirm'.

Paracelsus, in the *Book of Images*, speaks thus of the successive
colours of the Work: 'Although there are several elemental colours
—the colour blue belongs particularly to earth, green to water,
yellow to air and red to fire—yet the colours white and black refer
directly to the spagyric art, in which the four primitive colours,
i.e. black, white, yellow and red are also found. Black is, further,
the *root and origin* of the other colours; for every black matter may
be reverberated for the time necessary to it, in such a way that the
other three colours will appear in succession, each in turn. White
succeeds black, yellow succeeds white and red succeeds yellow.
And every matter reaching the fourth colour by means of the
reverberation is the *tincture* of things of its kind, that is to say of
its nature.'

In order to give some idea of the scope of this colour symbolism
and especially of the three major colours of the Work, we may note
that the *Virgin* is always represented draped in *blue* (corresponding
to black, as I shall show later), *God* in *white* and *Christ* in *red*.
These are the national colours of the French flag, which, moreover,
was invented by the mason, Louis David. In it the *dark blue or
black* represents the middle class; the white is reserved for the

people, the *pierrots* or peasants, and the red for the executive or royalty. In Chaldea, the Ziggurats, which were usually three-tiered towers, an example of which was the famous *Tower of Babel*, were faced in three colours: *black, white* and *reddish-purple*.

Up to now I have spoken theoretically about the colours, as the Masters have done before me, in order to act in accordance with the philosophical doctrine and with traditional usage. Perhaps it may now be in order to write for the benefit of the Sons of Science in a practical rather than a speculative way and thus to discover the difference between similitude and reality.

Few Philosophers have dared to venture on this slippery ground. Etteilla,[24] in describing a hermetic picture,[25] which he claims to have had in his possession, has preserved the legend, which appeared below it. Included, surprisingly enough, is the advice: 'Do not pay too much attention to the colour.' What does this mean? Can the ancient authors have been deceiving their readers deliberately? And what indication should the disciples of Hermes substitute for the discredited colours, in order to recognize and follow the right way?

Seek, my brothers, without becoming discouraged, since both here and at other obscure points you must make a great effort. You must have read in various parts of your works that the Philosophers speak clearly only when they want to divert the attention of the uniniated from their Round Table. The descriptions they give of their processes and the symbolical colours they attribute to them are of perfect clarity. Therefore, you may conclude that these observations, so fully described must be false and illusory. Your books are sealed, like the book of the Apocalypse; they are sealed with cabalistic seals. You must break them, one by one. The task is hard, I know, but to conquer without danger is to triumph without glory.

Learn, then, not how one colour differs from another, but rather how one process is to be distinguished from the one which follows it. And, first of all, what is a process? Quite simply, it is a way of

[24] Cf. *Le Denier du Pauvre* or *La Perfection des Métaux*. Paris, (about 1785), p. 58.
[25] This picture is said to have been painted towards the middle of the seventeenth century.

growing, tending and increasing the life which your stone has
received since its birth. This is a *modus operandi* which cannot
necessarily be translated by a succession of different colours. 'He
who knows the process,' writes Philalethes, 'will be honoured by the
princes and great ones of the earth.' And the same author adds:
'We do not hide anything from you, except the process.' However,
in order not to draw down upon my head the curse of the Philosophers, by revealing what they have thought it their duty to leave
hidden, I shall content myself with stating that the *process of the
stone*, that is to say its coction, *includes several others*, meaning
several repetitions of the same method of operation. Reflect, make
use of analogy, and, above all, do not desert the simple principles
of nature. Consider how you must eat every day in order to maintain your vitality; how sleep is indispensible to you, because it
promotes, on the one hand, the digestion and assimilation of food
and, on the other hand, the renewal of those cells used up by daily
work. What is more, must you not frequently excrete various waste
products, which cannot be assimilated?

In the same way, your stone needs nourishment in order to
increase its power and this nourishment must be graduated or even
changed at certain times. First give milk; the more substantial meat
diet will come later. And after each digestion, do not fail to remove
the excrements, since your stone could be infected by them. . . .
Follow nature in this way and obey her as faithfully as you can.
You will understand in what way it is fitting to carry out the
coction, when you have acquired perfect knowledge of the process.
In this way you will better understand Tollius'[26] admonition to the
puffers, those slaves to the literal meaning: 'Depart at once, you
who sedulously seek your diverse colours in your glass vessels.
You tire my ears with your black *crow*; you are as mad as that man
in the old story, who used to applaud at the theatre, although he
was there by himself, because he always imagined some new
spectacle before his eyes. You do the same, when you shed tears of
joy, when you imagine that you see in your vessels your white *dove*,
your yellow *eagle* and your red *pheasant*. Go away, I say, and keep

[26] J. Tollius, *Le Chemin du Ciel Chymique*. Trans. of *Manuductio ad
Coelum Chemicum*. Amstelaedami, Janss. Waesbergios, 1688.

XI.   NOTRE-DAME, PARIS—CENTRAL PORCH
The four Elements and the two Natures.

XII.   NOTRE-DAME, PARIS—CENTRAL PORCH
The Athenor and the Stone.

far from me, if you are seeking the philosophic stone in something fixed . . . for the latter will no more penetrate metal bodies than the body of a man will go through solid walls. . . .

'That is what I had to say to you about *colours*, so that in future you would leave off your useless tasks; to which I will add a word concerning smell.

'The Earth is black; Water is white; the Air becomes more yellow, the nearer it approaches the Sun; the Ether is completely red. In the same way, death is said to be black, life is full of light; the purer the light, the nearer it approaches the nature of the angels, who are pure spirits of fire. Now, is not the smell of death or a corpse unpleasant and disagreeable? So, with the Philosophers, a foul smell denotes fixation; a pleasant smell, on the other hand, indicates volatility, because it is nearer to life and warmth.'

To return to the base of the porch of Notre Dame, we shall find there, in the sixth place, the bas-relief of *Philosophy*, whose disc bears the figure of a cross. This is the expression of the four elements and the sign of the two metallic principles, *sun* and *moon*, or sulphur and mercury, which are, according to Hermes, the father and mother of the stone (pl. XI).

4

The motifs ornamenting the right side are less rewarding to decipher. They are blackened and worn away, having deteriorated mainly on account of the direction in which this part of the porch faces. Swept by the west winds, seven centuries of gales have worn some of them to the point where they are no more than blurred and indistinct outlines.

On the seventh bas-relief of the series—the first one on the right—we see a vertical section of the Athenor and the internal apparatus intended to support the Philosophers' egg. The human figure holds a stone in the right hand.

It is a griffin which is shown in the next circle. This mythical monster, whose head and chest are those of an eagle and which derives the rest of its body from the lion, teaches the investigator the conflicting qualities which he has to assemble in the philosophic matter (pl. XIII). In this picture we find the hieroglyph of the *first conjunction*, which only takes place little by little, at the same gradual pace as this painful and irksome task, which the Philosophers have called their *Eagles*. The series of operations, which, when complete, leads to the intimate union of sulphur and mercury, is also called *Sublimation*. It is by the repetition of the *Eagles* or *philosophic Sublimations*, that the exalted mercury frees itself of its gross and earthly parts, of its superfluous humidity, and takes possession of a portion of the fixed body, which it dissolves, absorbs and assimilates. *To make the eagle fly*, as the hermetic expression goes, is to extract light from the tomb and *bring it to the surface*— the characteristic of every *veritable sublimation*. This is what the fable of Theseus and Ariadne teaches us. In this case, Theseus is θεσ-ειος, the *organized, manifested light*, which is separated from *Ariadne*, the *spider* in the middle of its web—the empty *shell*, the *cocoon*, the *sheath of the butterfly* (Psyche). 'Know, my brother,' writes Philalethes,[27] 'that the exact preparation of the *flying Eagles* is the first degree of perfection and to know this requires an industrious and able spirit. . . . We have sweated and laboured much to arrive there, we have even passed sleepless nights. So you, who are only at the beginning, be sure that you will not succeed in the first operation without great labour. . . . 'Understand then, my brother, the words of the Wise and take note that they muster their eagles to devour the lion; and the fewer the eagles used, the fiercer the combat and the greater the difficulty in gaining the victory. In order to bring our Work to perfection, no less than *seven eagles* are needed and even *nine* should really be used. Our philosophic Mercury is the *bird of Hermes*, which is also called the *goose*, the *swan* and sometimes the *pheasant*.'

These are the *sublimations* described by Callimachus in the *Hymn to Delos* (v. 250. 255), when, speaking of *swans*, he says:

'The swans went round Delos *seven times* . . . and they had not yet sung the eighth time, when Apollo was born.'

[27] Lenglet-Dufresnoy, *Histoire de la Philosophie Hermétique. L'Entrée au Palais Fermé du Roy*, bk. II, p. 35. Paris, Coustelier, 1742.

XIII.   NOTRE-DAME, PARIS—CENTRAL PORCH
Conjunction of Sulphur and Mercury.

This is a variation of the procession which Joshua ordered *seven times* round Jericho, whose walls fell down before the eighth time (Joshua ch. VI, v. 16).

In order to indicate the violence of the combat, which precedes our conjunction, the Wise have used, as symbols of the *two natures*, the *Eagle* and the *Lion*, which are equal in power, but of contrary natures. The lion represents the terrestial and fixed force, while the eagle expresses the airy and volatile force. Coming face to face, the two champions attack and repulse one another and tear each other fiercely, until, the eagle having lost its wings and the lion its head, the antagonists form a single body, that of *animated mercury*, which is midway between their two natures and homogeneous in substance.

I remember long ago, when, as a student of the sublime Science, I was applying myself to this mystery so fraught with difficult riddles, I saw a fine house being built. Its decoration, reflecting as it did .my hermetic preoccupations, could not fail to surprise me. Above the main door were two young children, a boy and a girl, intertwined, drawing aside and lifting the veil which covered them. The top part of their bodies emerged from a mass of flowers, leaves and fruit. The corner was ornamented with a bas-relief, showing the symbolical combat between the eagle and the lion, which I have just mentioned. One can easily imagine that the architect had difficulty in placing such a bulky emblem, no doubt stipulated by his uncompromising client. . . .[28]

[28] This six-storey house, built of dressed stone, is situated in the seventeenth district, at the corner of the Boulevard Péreire and the Rue de Monbel. Similarly at Tousson, near Malesherbes (Seine-et-Oise), an old eighteenth century house of good appearance has engraved on its façade in lettering of the period the following inscription:

By a *labourer*
I was built
Disinterested and zealous,
He called me PIERRE BELLE (the beautiful stone)
In the year 1762

(Alchemy was still called *celestial agriculture* and its Adepts were called *Labourers*.)

The ninth subject gives us the opportunity of learning again the secret of making the *universal solvent*. In it a woman shows— allegorically—the materials necessary for the construction of the hermetic *vessel*. She holds up a small piece of wood looking rather like the stave of a barrel, the nature of which is revealed by the *oak* branch borne on the shield. Here again we find the *mysterious spring*, which is sculptured on the pier of the porch, but the gesture of the woman reveals the spirituality of this substance, this *fire of nature* (pl. XIV), without which nothing can grow down here. It is this spirit, spread over the surface of the globe, which the subtle and ingenious artist must capture as and when it appears. Also, I must add, a specific body is needed to serve as a receptacle; an attracting medium, containing a principle capable of receiving the spirit and 'embodying' it. 'Our bodies have roots in the air and heads on the ground' say the Wise. The spirit is the lodestone sealed in the belly of Aries, which must be seized with speed and skill at the moment of its birth.

'The water which we use,' writes the anonymous author of the *Clef du Cabinet Hermétique*, 'is a water containing all the virtues of heaven and earth; that is why it is the *general solvent of all Nature*. It is this which opens the doors of our royal hermetic chamber. In it, our king and our queen are shut up and thus it is their bath. . . . It is the Fountain of Trévisan, in which the King divests himself of his purple cloak, in order to clothe himself in black attire. . . . It is true that this water is difficult to possess. This is what makes the Cosmopolite say in his Enigma that it was rare in the island. . . . This author draws our attention to it more particularly by these words: "It is not like water from the clouds, although it has the same appearance." In another place, he describes it for us under the name of *steel* and *magnet*, since it is a veritable magnet, which attracts to itself all the influences of the sky, the sun, the moon and the stars, in order to transmit them to the earth. He says that this *steel* is found in *Aries*, which also marks the beginning of spring, when the sun passes through the sign of the *Ram* . . . Flamel gives us quite a correct picture of it in the *Figures d'Abraham le Juif*. He depicts for us an old, hollow oak,[29] from which proceeds

[29] Vide supra, p. 96.

XIV.   NOTRE-DAME, PARIS—CENTRAL PORCH
The Materials necessary for making the Solvent.

a fountain, whose water is being used by a gardener on the plants and flowers of a bed. The old *oak*, which is *hollow*, represents the *barrel* made of oak, in which he must putrefy the water to be used on the plants and which is much better than ordinary water. . . . Now, this is the place to reveal one of the great secrets of this Art, which Philosophers have hidden. This is the vessel, without which you cannot carry out the putrefaction and purification of our elements, any more than one can make wine without fermenting it in a cask. Now, as the barrel is made of oak, so the vessel must be of old oak, rounded inside like a half globe, whose sides are good and stout; failing which, two kegs, one over the other. Almost all philosophers have mentioned this *vessel*, which is absolutely necessary for this operation. Philalethes describes it by the fable of the snake Python, which Cadmus pierced through and through against an oak tree. There is a figure in the book of the *Douze Clefs*[30] representing this same operation and the *vessel* in which it takes place. Out of this proceeds a great cloud of smoke, marking the fermentation and bubbling of this water. This smoke ends at a window, where the sky is to be seen. In the sky are depicted the sun and moon, showing the *origin of this water* and the virtues which it contains. It is our *mercurial vinegar*, which comes down from the sky to the earth and which rises from the earth to the sky.'

We have given the text of this, because it can be of use, providing always that one knows how to read with prudence and understand with wisdom. Here it is a case of repeating again that maxim, so dear to the Adepts; the spirit gives life, but the letter kills.

We are faced with an extremely complex symbol, that of the lion. It is complex because, in view of the present bare state of the stone, we cannot be content with a single explanation. The Wise have given various titles to the lion, either to express the aspect of the substances they were processing or to emphasize a special and preponderant aspect of them. In the emblem of the Griffin (eighth motif), we saw that the lion, king of the earthly beasts, represented the fixed, basic part of a compound, which, when in contact with opposing volatility, lost the better part of itself. That is to say it lost

[30] Cf. the *Douze Clefs de la Philosophie* of Basil Valentine. Paris, Moet, 1659, clef 12. (Re-edited by the Editions de Minuit, 1956.)

the part which characterized its form, or, in hieroglyphic language, its head. This time we have to study the animal by itself and we do not know in what colour it was originally painted. Generally the *lion* is the *sign of gold*, both alchemical and natural. It thus represents the physico-chemical properties of these substances. But the texts give the same name to the matter which is receptive of the *universal spirit*, the *secret fire*, during processing of the solvent. In both these cases it represents power, incorruptability and perfection, these being further indicated clearly enough by the warrior with drawn sword, the mail-clad knight, displaying the king of the alchemical bestiary (pl. XV).

The first magnetic agent which is used to prepare the solvent— designated, by some, Alkahest—is called the *green Lion*, not so much because it is green in colour as because it has not yet acquired those mineral characteristics, which in chemistry distinguish the adult state from the nascent one. It is a *green and sour* fruit, compared with the *red, ripe* fruit. It is metallic youth on which Evolution has not yet worked, but which contains the latent germ of real energy, which will be called upon to develop later. It is arsenic and lead in respect of silver and gold. It is present imperfection from which the great future perfection will emerge; the rudiment of our embryo, the embryo of our stone, the stone of our Elixir. Certain Adepts, Basil Valentine among them, have called it *green vitriol*, in order to reveal its hot, burning and salty nature. Others have called it the *Philosophers' Emerald*, the *Dew of May*, the *Herb of Saturn*, the *Vegetable Stone*, etc. 'Our water takes the name of the leaves of all the trees, of the trees themselves, and of everything green in colour, in order to mislead the foolish,' says Master Arnold of Villanova.

As for the *Red Lion*, according to the Philosophers it is nothing more than the same matter, or the *Green Lion*, brought by certain processes to this special quality which characterizes hermetic gold or the *Red Lion*. This has led Basil Valentine to give the following advice: 'Dissolve and nourish the real lion with the blood of the green lion, since the fixed blood of the red Lion is made from the volatile blood of the green one, which makes them both of the same nature.'

XV.   NOTRE-DAME, PARIS—CENTRAL PORCH
The fixed Body.

XVI. NOTRE-DAME, PARIS—CENTRAL PORCH
Union of the Fixed and the Volatile.

Of these interpretations, which is the true one? I must confess that this is a question which I am unable to solve. Without doubt, this symbolical lion was either painted or gilded. Any trace of cinnabar, of malachite or of metal would immediately resolve our doubts; but nothing remains but the worn and defaced grey limestone. The stone lion preserves his secret!

The extraction of the red and incombustible sulphur is shown by the figure of a monster, which combines the form of both cock and fox. It is the same symbol used by Basil Valentine in the third of his *Douze Clefs*. 'It is the splendid cloak with the salt of the Stars,' says the Adept, 'which follows this celestial sulphur, closely guarded for fear it might be spoilt, and makes them fly like a bird, when the need arises. The cock will eat the fox and will be drowned and suffocated in the water. Then, regaining life from the fire, it will be devoured by the fox, (in order that each may have its turn). (pl. XVI).

The fox-cock is succeeded by the *Bull* (pl. XVII). Considered as a sign of the zodiac, this is the second month of the preparatory operations in the first work, and the first process of the elementary fire in the second. Since the bull and the ox were sacred to the sun, just as the cow was to the moon, the bull as a symbol represents Sulphur, the male principle, the sun being described by Hermes as the Father of the Stone. The bull and the cow, the sun and the moon, sulphur and mercury, are thus hieroglyphs identical in meaning and designating the primitive, contrary natures *before their conjunction*. These natures are extracted by the Art from imperfect mixtures.

5

Of the twelve medallions, which ornament the lower row of the base, we shall concentrate on ten, since two of the subjects have been too badly mutilated to re-establish their meaning. We will, therefore, regretfully pass over the formless remains of the fifth medallion (on the left side) and the eleventh (on the right side).

Next to the pier which separates the central porch from the

north portal the first motif shows an unhorsed knight clinging to the mane of a spirited horse (pl. XVIII). This allegory concerns the extraction of the fixed central and pure parts by the volatile or etheric ones, in the philosophical *Dissolution*. More exactly, it is the rectification of the spirit obtained and the action of this spirit on the heavy matter. The charger, the symbol of speed and lightness, represents the spiritual substance; its rider shows the weightiness of the gross, metallic body. At each cohobation,[31] the horse throws its rider, the volatile leaves the fixed; but the horseman immediately reasserts his right, until the exhausted animal, now vanquished and submissive, agrees to carry this stubborn burden and cannot again free itself from it. The absorption of the fixed by the volatile is carried out slowly and with difficulty. Success needs much patience and perseverence and the repeated outpouring of water on the earth, of spirit on the body. It is only by this technique, truly a long and tedious one, that one can succeed in extracting the occult *salt* from the *red lion*, helped by the spirit of the *green lion*. The charger of Notre Dame is the same as the winged Pegasus of the fable (root πηγη, source), which, like the charger, throws its riders, whether they are called Perseus or Bellerophon. It is also the one which transports *Perseus* through the air to the *Hesperides* and which, with a blow of its hoof makes the *fountain Hippocrene* flow on Mount Helicon. This fountain, it is said, was discovered by Cadmus.

On the second medallion, the Initiate holds up a *mirror* in one hand, while with the other he holds up the horn of Amalthea (pl. XIX). Beside him is seen the *Tree of Life*. The mirror symbolizes the beginning of the work, the Tree of Life marks its end and the horn of plenty the result.

Alchemically, the first matter, the one which the artist must choose in order to begin the work, is called the *Mirror of the Art*. 'Commonly among the Philosophers', says Moras de Respour,[32] 'it is known as the *Mirror of Art* because it is principally through

---

[31] *Translator's note:* Cohobation is the process of returning a distillate to its residue and then redistilling.

[32] De Respour, *Rares Expériences sur l'Esprit minéral*. Paris, Langlois et Barbin, 1668.

XVII.   NOTRE-DAME, PARIS—CENTRAL PORCH
Philosophic Sulphur.

XVIII.   NOTRE-DAME, PARIS—CENTRAL PORCH
Cohobation.

XIX.   NOTRE-DAME, PARIS—CENTRAL PORCH
Origin and Result of the Stone.

XX. NOTRE-DAME, PARIS—CENTRAL PORCH
The Knowledge of Weights.

it that the composition of metals in the veins of the earth has been learnt. . . . Also it has been said that the indication of nature alone can instruct us.' This is exactly what the Cosmopolite[33] also teaches, when he says, in speaking of Sulphur: 'In its kingdom there is a mirror in which the whole world is seen. Anyone looking in this mirror can see and learn the three parts of the Wisdom of the whole world and in this way he will become very wise in these three kingdoms, as were Aristotle, Avicenna and many others. They, like their predecessors, saw in this *mirror* how the world had been created.' Basil Valentine, in his *Testamentum*, writes similarly: 'The whole body of the *Vitriol* must be recognized only as a *Mirror of the philosophical Science*. . . . It is a Mirror in which you see our Mercury, our Sun and Moon, appear and shine; by which you can show in an instant and prove to Doubting Thomas the blindness of his crass ignorance.' Pernety does not mention this term in his *Dictionnaire Mytho-hermétique*, either because he did not know it, or because he voluntarily omitted it. This so common and so much despised subject becomes later the *Tree of Life*; the Elixir or the Philosophers' Stone; nature's masterpiece, aided by human industry; the pure and rich jewel of alchemy. It is an aboslute metallic synthesis and assures for the fortunate owner of this treasure the triple endowment of knowledge, fortune and health. It is the horn of plenty, the inexhaustible source of material happiness in our terrestial world. Let us finally remember that the *mirror* is the attribute of *Truth, Prudence* and *Knowledge* to all the Greek poets and mythologists.

Next comes the allegory of the *weight of nature*, in which the alchemist draws back the veil, covering the scales (pl. XX).

None of the philosophers has had much to say about the secret of weights. Basil Valentine has been content to remark that it was necessary 'to give a white swan for a man twice fired', which would correspond to the *Sigillum Sapientum* of Huginus à Barma. Here the artist holds a balance, with one scale outweighing the other in the apparent ratio of two to one. The Cosmopolite, in his *Treatise on Salt* is even less precise: 'The weight of the water,' he says, 'must

[33] *Nouvelle Lumière chymique. Traité du Soufre*, p. 78. Paris, d'Houry, 1649.

G

be plural, and that of the earth, coloured white or red, must be singular.' The author of the *Aphorismes Basiliens* or the *Canons Hermétiques de l'Esprit et de l'Ame*[34] writes in Canon XVI: 'We begin our hermetic work with the conjunction of the three principles, consisting in the weight of the body, which must with its half almost equal the spirit and the soul.' If Raymond Lully and Philalethes have spoken of it, many have preferred to keep silent; some have claimed that nature alone apportions the quantities according to a mysterious harmony, unknown to the Art. These contradictions are only apparent. In reality, we know that philosophic mercury results from the absorption of a certain part of sulphur by a determined quantity of mercury; it is, thus, essential to know exactly the reciprocal proportions of the components, if one is following the old way. I need not add that these proportions are wrapped up in similes and covered with obscurity, even by the most sincere authors. But one should note, on the other hand, that it is possible to substitute common gold for metallic sulphur. In this case, since the excess solvent can always be separated by distillation, the weight is brought back to a simple appreciation of consistency. You can see that the scales are a valuable indication for determining the old way, in which it was apparently necessary to exclude gold. I mean common gold, which has undergone neither exaltation nor transfusion, the operations which, by modifying its properties and its physical characteristics, render it fit for the work.

A special and little-used solution is expressed by one of the cartouches, which we are studying. It is the solution of ordinary quicksilver, in order to obtain from it the *common mercury* of the Philosophers, which the latter call 'our mercury', so as to differentiate it from the liquid metal from which it comes. Although one can often find quite lengthy descriptions on this subject, I will not hide the fact that such an operation appears to me hazardous, if not dubious. In the minds of those authors who have spoken of it, ordinary mercury, relieved of all impurity and perfectly exalted, would take on a fiery quality, which it does not possess, and would be capable of becoming a solvent in its turn. A queen seated on a

[34] Printed following the *Oeuvres tant Médicinales que Chymiques*, of R.P. de Castaigne. Paris, de la Nove, 1681.

XXI.   NOTRE-DAME, PARIS—CENTRAL PORCH
The Queen kicks down Mercury, Servus Fugitivus.

XXII.   NOTRE-DAME, PARIS—CENTRAL PORCH
The Reign of Saturn.

throne kicks over the servant, who comes with a cup in his hand to offer her his services (pl. XXI). One should, therefore, see in this technique—supposing that it could supply the desired solvent—only a modification of the old way, and not a special practice, since the agent always remains the same. Furthermore, I do not see what advantage could be gained from a solution of mercury obtained with the aid of the philosophic solvent, when the latter is the chief and secret agent par excellence. This, however, is what Sabine Stuart de Chevalier[35] claims:

'In order to have the *philosophic mercury*,' writes this author, 'it is necessary to dissolve ordinary mercury without diminishing any of its weight, since the whole of its substance must be converted into philosophic water. The philosophers know of a natural fire, which penetrates right to the heart of the mercury and which destroys it internally. They also know of a solvent, which converts it into pure and natural silver water. This water does not contain, nor must it contain, any corrosive. As soon as the mercury is freed from its bonds and is overcome by the heat, it takes the form of water, and this same water is the most precious thing in the world. Very little time is necessary to make ordinary mercury take this form.' I must be excused for not being of the same opinion, since I have good reasons, based on experience, for believing[36] that ordinary mercury, deprived of a proper agent, could become a *water* useful for the Work. The *servus fugitivus* which we need is a solid, brittle *mineral* and metallic *water*, having the aspect of a *stone* and very easily liquified. It is this *water*, *coagulated* in the form of a stony mass, which is the *Alkahest* and *universal solvent*. If it is right, as Philalethes counsels, to read the Philosophers with a grain of salt, then the whole salt cellar should be used when studying Stuart de Chevalier.

An old man, stiff with cold, is bent under the arc of the next medallion. Weak and feeble, he is leaning on a block of stone, his left hand hidden in a sort of muff (pl. XXII).

[35] Sabine Stuart de Chevalier, *Discours philosophiques sur les Trois Principes* or the *Clef du Sanctuaire philosophique*. Paris, Quillau, 1781.
[36] *Translator's note:* The question would seem to arise as to whether 'believing' is a misprint. The sense would seem to require 'disbelieving'.

It is easy to recognize here the first phase of the second work, when the hermetic *Rebis*, enclosed in the centre of the Athenor, suffers the dislocation of its parts and tends to be mortified. It is the active and gentle beginning of the *fire of the wheel*, symbolized by cold and by winter, the embryonic season when the seeds, shut up in the womb of the philosophic earth, are subject to the fermentative influence of humidity. It is the *reign of Saturn*, which is going to appear, the emblem of radical dissolution, of decomposition and of the colour black. 'I am old, weak and sick', Basil Valentine makes him say, 'for this reason I am shut up in a grave. . . . The fire torments me greatly and death tears at my skin and my bones.' Demetrius, a traveller quoted by Plutarch—the Greeks beat everyone, even at bragging—relates seriously that, in one of the islands which he visited off the coast of England, Saturn was imprisoned and wrapped in a deep sleep. The giant Briareus (Aegaeon) was the jailor of his prison. Thus did famous authors write history with the help of hermetic fables!

The sixth medallion is just a fragmentary repetition of the second one. The Adept is seen with his hands joined in an attitude of prayer and seems to be addressing thanksgiving to Nature, shown as the head and shoulders of a woman reflected in a *mirror*. We recognize the hieroglyph as showing the *subject of the Wise*, the mirror in which 'one sees the whole of nature disclosed' (pl. XXIII).

On the right of the porch, the seventh medallion shows us an old man ready to cross the threshold of the *Mysterious Palace*. He has just torn down the awning, which hid the entrance from the eyes of the uninitiated. The first step in the practice has been achieved, the discovery of the agent capable of carrying out the reduction of the fixed body, of reincruding[37] it, according to the accepted expression, in a form analogous to that of its first substance (pl. XXIV). The alchemists are alluding to this operation, when they speak of *reanimating the corporifications*, that is to say giving life to the dead metals. It is Philalethes' *Entrance to the Closed Palace of the King* and Ripley's and Basil Valentine's first door, which one must

[37] To reincrude—technical hermetic term, meaning to render raw, to put back to a state previous to the one characterizing maturity, to retrogress.

XXIII.   NOTRE-DAME, PARIS—CENTRAL PORCH
The Subject of the Wise.

XXIV.   NOTRE-DAME, PARIS—CENTRAL PORCH
The Entrance to the Sanctuary.

know how to open. The old man is none other than our Mercury, the secret agent, whose nature, method of action, materials and time of preparation have been revealed to us in several bas-reliefs. As for the Palace, it represents the living, philosophic or base gold, despised by the ignorant and hidden under the rags, which conceal it from our eyes, although it is extremely precious to one who knows its value. In this motif, we see a variation of the allegory of the *green and red lions*, of the solvent and the body to be dissolved. Indeed the old man, whom the texts indentify with Saturn—who, it is said, ate his children—was formerly painted green, while the interior of the palace showed a purple colouring. I shall say later to what source one may refer, in order to re-establish the meaning of all these figures, by means of the original colours. It should also be noted that the hieroglyph of Saturn, considered as a solvent, is very ancient. On a sarcophagus at the Louvre, which had contained the mummy of a hierophant priest of Thebes named Poeris, the god Shu can be seen on the left hand side, holding up the sky, with the aid of the god Chnouphis (the soul of the world), while at their feet crouches the god Ser (Saturn), whose skin is *green in colour*.

The next circle enables us to witness the encounter of the old man and the crowned king; the solvent and the body; the volatile principle and the fixed metallic salt, which is incombustible and pure. This allegory has much in common with the parable of Bernard Trévisan, in which the 'ancient and aged priest' shows himself so well acquainted with the properties of the occult fountain and its action on the 'king of the country' whom it loves, attracts and swallows up. In this method and at the time when the mercury is animated, the gold or king is dissolved little by little and without violence; this is not so in the second method, in which, contrary to ordinary amalgamation, the hermetic mercury seems to attack the metal with characteristic vigour, closely resembling chemical effervescence. The wise have said, with reference to this, that in the Conjunction violent storms arose and the waves of the sea presented the spectacle of a bitter 'combat'. Some have represented this reaction by the fight to the death of dissimilar animals: *the eagle and the lion* (Nicholas Flamel); the cock and the fox (Basil Valentine); etc. But in my opinion the best description—certainly the most initiatory one—is that given by that great philosopher, Cyrano de Bergerac, of the terrible duel between *the remora and the salamander,* which took place before his very eyes. Others, and they are the most numerous, have drawn upon the traditional accounts of creation for their similes. They have described the formation of the philosophical compound by comparing it to that of the terrestial chaos, which results from the upheavals and reactions of fire and water, air and earth.

The style of Notre Dame is no less noble and expressive for being more human and more familiar. Here, the two natures are represented by aggressive and quarrelsome children, who have come to blows and hit each other unsparingly. At the height of the fray, one of them drops a pot and the other a stone (pl. XXV). It would scarcely be possible to describe more clearly or simply the action of the *pontic water* on the heavy matter and this medallion does great credit to the master who conceived it.

In this series of subjects, with which we will conclude the description of the figures of the great porch, it clearly appears that the guiding principle was to group the various points in the practice of the Solution. Indeed, it alone suffices to identify the way which has been taken; the solution of alchemical gold by the solvent Alkahest characterizes the first way; that of common gold by *our mercury,* indicates the second. By the latter, *animated mercury* is obtained.

Finally, a second solution, the solution of red or white Sulphur by the philosophic water, is the subject of the twelfth and last basrelief. A warrior drops his sword and stops speechless in front of a tree, at the foot of which a ram is rising up. The tree bears three enormous fruits like balls and the silhouette of a bird is seen coming out of the branches. Here one recognizes the *solar tree,* described by the Cosmopolite in the parable from the *Traité de la Nature,* the tree from which water must be extracted. As for the warrior, he represents the artist, who has just accomplished the *labour of Hercules*—our preparation. The *ram* shows that he has chosen a favourable season and the right substance. The bird indicates the volatile nature of the compound 'more celestial than terrestrial'. Now nothing remains for him but to imitate Saturn, who, says the Cosmopolite, 'drew ten parts of this water and immediately picked the

XXV. NOTRE-DAME, PARIS—CENTRAL PORCH
Dissolution. Combat of the two Natures.

fruit of the solar tree and put it in this water. . . . For this water is the *Water of Life*, which has the power to improve the fruits of this tree, so that from then on there will be no further need to plant or graft any, because by its scent alone it can make the six other trees assume the same nature as itself.' In addition, this picture is a replica of the famous expedition of the Argonauts. There we see Jason with the ram with the golden fleece and the tree with the precious fruits of the garden of the Hesperides.

In the course of this study, we had occasion to regret both the ravages of foolish iconoclasts and the total disappearance of the colours which our splendid cathedral used to possess. There is no document left in any library, which could be of assistance to the investigator or remedy, even partially, the ravages of the centuries. However, there is no need to pore over old parchments or thumb through ancient prints. Notre Dame itself preserves the original colouring of the figures of its great porch.

Guillaume de Paris, whose perspicacity we must bless, was able to forsee the great damage which time would do to his work. Like the wise master that he was, he had the motifs of the medallions reproduced on the panes of the central rose window. Thus glass complements stone and, thanks to the help of the fragile material, the hidden meaning regains its first purity.

The doubtful points of the statues can be resolved there. For example, in the allegory of the Cohobation (first medallion), the glass shows no ordinary horseman, but a prince crowned in gold, in white tunic and red hose. One of the two fighting boys is in green, the other in violet grey. The queen striking down Mercury wears a white crown, a green gown and a purple cloak. One is even surprised to see there some pictures which have disappeared from the façade. For example, this workman seated at a red table, pulling large pieces of gold out of a sack; this woman, in a green bodice and wearing a scarlet tunic, doing her hair in a mirror; these heavenly twins of the lesser zodiac, one of which is made of ruby and the other of emerald, etc.

What a profound subject for meditation is offered to us by our ancestral hermetic Idea, in all its harmony and unity! In stone on the façade, in glass in the enormous orb of the rose window, it passes from silence to revelation, from solemnity to excitement, from inertia to vivid expression. Solid, worn and cold in the crude light outside, it flashes into multicoloured facets from the crystal and permeates through the nave, vibrant, warm, diaphanous and pure as Truth itself.

The spirit cannot but feel troubled in the presence of this even more paradoxical antithesis: the torch of alchemical thought illuminating the temple of Christian thought.

Let us leave the great porch and proceed to the north portal or Portal of the Virgin.

In the centre of the tympanum on the middle cornice, observe the sarcophagus which figures in an episode in the life of Christ. On it you will see seven circles. These are the symbols of the seven planetary metals (pl. XXVI):

> The Sun indicates gold, Mercury quicksilver;
> As Saturn stands for lead, so Venus stands for copper,
> The Moon for silver, Jupiter for tin,
> And Mars for iron.[38]

The central circle is decorated in a particular way, while the other six are repeated, two by two—something which never happens in the purely decorative motifs of gothic art. What is more, this symmetry goes from the centre towards the ends, as the Cosmopolite teaches: 'Look at the sky and the spheres of the planets,' says this author,[39] 'you will see that Saturn is the highest of all, succeeded by Jupiter and then by Mars, the Sun, Venus, Mercury and finally the Moon. Consider now that the virtues of the planets do not ascend, but descend. Experience itself teaches us that Mars can easily be converted into Venus, but not Venus into Mars— Venus being a lower sphere. Similarly Jupiter is easily transmuted into Mercury, because Jupiter is higher than Mercury. The former is the second below the firmament, the latter second above the earth. Saturn is the highest, the moon the lowest. The sun mixes with all

[38] *La Cabale Intellective.* Mss. of the Bibliothèque de l'Arsenal, S. et A. 72, p. 15.
[39] *Nouvelle Lumière chymique. Traité du Mercure,* chap. IX, p. 41. Paris, Jean d'Houry.

XXVI.   NOTRE-DAME, PARIS—PORTAL OF THE VIRGIN
The Planetary Metals.

XXVII.   NOTRE-DAME, PARIS—PORTAL OF THE VIRGIN
The Dog and the Doves.

of them, but is never improved by the inferior ones. Further, you will note that there is a great correspondence between Saturn and the Moon, with the Sun midway between them. There is also a correspondence between Mercury and Jupiter and between Mars and Venus. In the midst of all is the Sun.'

The pattern of possible changes among metallic planets is thus shown on the porch of Notre Dame in the most formal manner. The central motif symbolizes the Sun; the roses at the ends indicate Saturn and the Moon; then come Jupiter and Mercury respectively; finally, on either side of the Sun, are Mars and Venus.

But more is to come. If we analyse this strange line, which seems to unite the circumferences of the roses, we see that it is formed of a succession of four crosses and three crosiers, one of which has a single spiral and the other two double spirals. Note, in passing, that here too if only ornamentation was intended, then six or eight attributes would be necessary in order to maintain perfect symmetry. This is not the case and proof that the symbolical meaning was intended is given by the fact that one space—that on the left— remains empty.

The four crosses, as in the spagyric notation, represent the imperfect metals; the crosiers with double spirals the two perfect ones and the simple crosier represents Mercury, which is half metal, or semi-perfect.

But if, leaving the tympanum, we lower our eyes to the left part of the base, divided into five niches, we shall notice between the outer curves of the arches some curious figurines.

Going from the outside towards the right, we find the *dog* and the two *doves* (pl. XXVII) revealed in the animation of exalted mercury. This is the *dog of Corascene*, which Artephius and Philalethes say one must know how to separate from the compost in the state of black powder. These are the *Doves of Diana*, another hopeless enigma, hiding the spiritualization and sublimation of philosophical mercury. These are followed by the *lamb*, emblem of the purification of the arsenical principle of the matter. Then comes the *man turning round*, who well illustrates that alchemical maxim *solve et coagula*, which teaches how to achieve the elementary conversion by violatilizing the fixed and fixing the volatile (pl. XXVIII).

If you know how to dissolve the fixed,
And to make the dissolved fly,
Then to fix the flying in powder,
You have something to console yourself with.

In this part of the porch, a sculpture of the *crow*, the chief hieroglyph of our practice, was once to be found. The crow of Notre Dame, the principal figure of the hermetic coat of arms, has at all times exerted a powerful attraction on the vulgar herd of puffers. This was because, according to ancient legend, it was the only clue to a sacred hoard. The story goes that Guillaume de Paris, 'who,' said Victor Hugo, 'was doubtless damned for having added such an infernal frontispiece to the holy poem eternally sung by the rest of the building,' had hidden the philosophers' stone under one of the pillars of the huge nave. And the exact spot of this mysterious hiding-place was precisely determined by the angle of vision of the crow. . . .

So in former times, according to the legend, the symbolic bird marked externally the unknown position of the secret pillar, where the treasure was supposed to be concealed.

On the external surface of the pillars, supporting the lintel, the signs of the zodiac are represented. Beginning from the bottom, you find first of all *Aries*, then *Taurus* and above that *Gemini*. These are the months of spring, indicating the beginning of the work and the propitious time for operations.

The objection will no doubt be made that the zodiac cannot have any occult significance and that it represents quite simply the path of the constellations. This is possible. But in that case we should have to find the astronomical order, the cosmic succession of the signs of the zodiac, which was certainly known to our Ancestors. However, here *Leo* succeeds *Gemini*, thus usurping the place of *Cancer*, which is to be found rejected on the opposite pillar. The *imager*, therefore, intended, by this cunning transposition, to indicate the conjunction of the philosophic ferment—or the Lion—with the mercurial compound, a union which must be achieved towards the end of the fourth month of the first Work.

Under this porch, there is to be seen a small, square bas-relief,

XXVIII.   NOTRE-DAME, PARIS—PORTAL OF THE VIRGIN
"Solve et Coagula".

XXIX.   NOTRE-DAME, PARIS—PORTAL OF THE VIRGIN
The Bath of the Stars. Condensation of the Universal Spirit.

which is really curious. It synthesises and expresses the *condensation of the universal Spirit*, which, as soon as it is materialized, forms the famous *Bath of the Stars*, in which the chemical sun and moon must bathe, change their natures and become rejuvenated. Here we see a child falling from a crucible as large as a jar. This is supported by a standing archangel with a halo and outspread wing, who appears to be striking the innocent. The whole background of the composition is occupied by a night sky studded with stars (pl. XXIX). We recognize in this subject a very simplified form of the allegory, dear to Nicholas Flamel, of the *Massacre of the Innocents*, which we shall soon see on a window pane of the Sainte Chapelle.

Without entering into details of the operative techniques—which no author has dared to do—I will, however, say that the *universal Spirit*, embodied in minerals under the alchemical name of *Sulphur* constitutes the principle and the effective agent of all metallic tinctures. But one cannot obtain this *Spirit*, the red blood of the children, except by decomposing what nature had first assembled in them. It is, therefore, necessary that the body should perish, that it should be crucified and should die, if one wishes to extract the *soul*, the *metallic life* and the *celestial Dew* imprisoned therein. And this quintessence, transfused into a pure, fixed and perfectly digested body, will give birth to a new creature, more splendid than any of those from which it proceeds. The bodies have no action on one another; the spirit alone is active.

That is why, knowing that the mineral blood, which they needed to animate the fixed and inert body of gold, was nothing but a condensation of the universal Spirit, the soul of all things; that this condensation in its humid form, capable of penetrating sublunary mixtures and making them grow, was accomplished only by night, under the protection of darkness, a clear sky and calm air; and finally that the season when it was manifested with most activity and abundance corresponded to springtime on earth; for all these reasons, the Wise gave it the name of the *Dew of May*. Similarly we are not surprised to find Thomas Corneille[40] asserting that the great masters of the Rose-Cross were called *Frerès de la Rosée*

[40] Dictionnaire des *Arts et des Sciences*, art. Rose-Croix. Paris, Coignard, 1731.

Cuite (Brothers of the boiled dew), a meaning which they themselves gave to the initials of their order, F.R.C.

I would like to be able to say more on this extremely important
subject and to show how the *Dew of May* (Maia was the mother of
Hermes)—the life-giving humidity of the month of *Mary, the Virgin
Mother*—can easily be extracted from a particular body, which is
abject and despised and whose characteristics I have already described. There are, however, bounds which may not be over-
stepped. . . . We are touching on the greatest secret of the Work
and I must remain true to my vow. It is the *Verbum dimissum* of
Trévisan, the *Lost Word* of the medieval freemasons, what all the
hermetic fraternities were hoping to find. Its discovery was the aim
of all their work and the raison d'être of their existence.[41] *Post
tenebras lux.* Let us not forget that light comes out of darkness.
Light is diffuse in obscurity, in blackness, as day is in the night.
It was from the darkness of *Chaos* that light was extracted and its
radiation assembled. If, on the day of Creation, the divine Spirit
moved on the waters of the Abyss—*Spiritus Domini ferebatur super
aquas*—this invisible spirit could not at first be distinguished from
the watery mass and was confused with it.

Finally, remember that God took *six days* to perfect his Great
Work; that the light was separated out on the first day and that the
following days, like our own, were marked by regular and altern-
ating intervals of darkness and light:

> At *midnight* a *Virgin mother*
> Brings forth this *shining star;*
> At this miraculous moment,
> We call God our brother.

[41] Among the most celebrated centres of initiation of this kind, I
would mention the orders of the *Illuminates,* the *Knights of the Black
Eagle,* of the *Two Eagles,* of the *Apocalypse;* the *Initiate Brothers of
Asia,* of *Palestine,* of the *Zodiac;* the Societies of the *Black Brothers,* of
the *Elected Coens,* of the *Mopses,* of the *Seven Swords,* of the *Invisible
Ones,* of the *Princes of Death;* the *Knights of the Swan (instituted by
Elias),* the *Knights of the Dog and the Cock, the Knights of the Round
Table,* of the *Genet,* of the *Thistle,* of the *Bath,* of the *Dead Beast,* of the
Amaranth, etc.

6

Let us retrace our steps and pause at the south portal, still called the Porch of St. Anne. It offers us only a single motif, but the interest of this is considerable, because it describes the shortest practice of our Science and among lessons in stone it therefore deserves pride of place.

'See,' says Grillot de Givry,[42] 'sculptured on the right portal of Notre Dame of Paris, the bishop perched above an athenor, where the philosophical mercury, chained in limbo, is being sublimated. It teaches the origin of the sacred fire; and the Chapter of the cathedral, by leaving this door closed all the year in accordance with a secular tradition, shows that this is *not the vulgar way*, but one unknown to the crowd and reserved for the small number of the elite of Wisdom.'[43]

Few alchemists will admit the possibility of *two ways*, one short and easy, called the *dry way*, the other, longer and less rewarding, called the *moist way*. This may be due to the fact that many authors deal exclusively with the longer process, either because they do not know of the other, or because they prefer to remain silent about it, rather than to teach its principles. Pernety refuses to believe in those alternative methods, while Huginus à Barma, on the contrary, asserts that the ancient masters, such as Geber, Lully and Paracelsus, each had his own particular process.

Chemically speaking, there is no objection to a method, employing the moist way, being replaced by another, which makes use of dry reactions, in order to arrive at the same result. Hermetically the emblem we are studying is a proof of this. We shall find a second one in the eighteenth-century Encyclopaedia, where the assurance is given that the Great Work may be accomplished in two ways; one, called the moist way, being longer but held more in honour and the

[42] Grillot de Givry, *Le Grand Oeuvre*. Paris, Chacornac, 1907, p. 27.

[43] At St. Peter's, Rome, the same door, called the Holy Door or Jubilee Door, is gilded and walled up. Once every twenty-five years, or four times in a century, the Pope opens it with a hammer.

other, or dry way, being much less esteemed. In the latter 'the *celestial Salt*, which is the Philosophers' mercury, must be boiled for four days in a crucible over a naked fire, together with a terrestial metallic body.'

In the second part of the work, attributed to Basil Valentine,[44] but which seems rather to be by Senior Zadith, the author appears to have the dry way in mind when he writes that 'in order to arrive at this Art, neither great labour nor trouble is required and the expenses are small, the instruments of little worth. For this Art may be learnt in less than twelve hours and brought to perfection within the space of *eight days*, if it has its own principle within itself.'

Philalethes, in chapter XIX of the *Introitus*, after having spoken of the long way, which he describes as tiresome and good only for rich people, says: 'But by our way no more than *a week* is necessary; God has reserved this rare and easy way for the despised poor and for abject saints.' Furthermore, Langlet-Dufresnoy, in his *Remarques* on this chapter, thinks that 'this way is achieved by the *double* philosophical *mercury*' and adds: 'The work is thereby accomplished in *eight days*, instead of taking nearly eighteen months by the first way.'

This shortened way, which is, however, covered by a thick veil, has been called by the Wise the *Regime of Saturn*. The boiling of the Work, instead of necessitating the use of a glass vase, requires only the help of a simple crucible. 'I will stir up your body in an earthenware vase, in which I will inter it', writes a famous author,[45] who says again further on: 'Make a fire in your glass, that is to say in the earth which holds it enclosed. This brief method, about which we have freely instructed you, seems to me to be the shorter way and the true philosophical sublimation, in order to arrive at the perfection of this difficult task.' This could be the explanation of the basic maxim of our Science: *'One single vessel, one single matter, one single furnace.'*

[44] *Azoth ou Moyen de faire l'Or caché des Philosophes.* Paris, Pierre Moet, 1659, p. 140.

[45] Salomon Trismosin, *La Toyson d'Or.* Paris, Ch. Sevestre, 1612, p. 72 and 100.

In the preface to his book,[46] Cyliani refers to the two processes in these terms: 'I would like to warn you here never to forget that only two matters of the same origin are needed, the one volatile, the other fixed; that there are *two ways*, the dry way and the moist way. I follow the latter one for preference *as my duty* although the former is very familiar to me: it is done with a single matter.'

Henri de Lintaut also gives a favourable testimonial to the dry way when he writes:[47] 'This secret surpasses all the secrets in the world, for by it you can in a *short time*, without great trouble or labour, arrive at a great transmutation. For information about this, see Isaac Hollandois, who speaks of it more fully.' Unfortunately our author is no more forthcoming than his colleagues. 'When I consider,' writes Henckel,[48] 'that the artist Elias, quoted by Helvetius, claims that the preparation of the Philosophic stone is begun and finished in the space of *four days*, and that he has actually shown this stone, still adhering to the fragments of the *crucible*, it seems to me that it would not be so absurd to ask whether what the alchemists call great months may not be as many days, which would mean a very limited space of time. And to ask further whether there may not be a method, which consists only in keeping the matters in the greatest degree of fluidity for a long time, which could be achieved by a violent fire, maintained by the action of the bellows. However, this method cannot be carried out in all laboratories and perhaps not everyone would find it practicable.'

The hermetic emblem of Notre Dame, which already in the seventeenth century had attracted the attention of the knowledgeable De Laborde,[49] occupies the pier of the porch, from the base to the architrave, and is sculptured in detail on the three sides of the engaged pillar. It is a tall, noble statue of St. Marcellus with mitred head, surmounted by a canopy with turrets, and, as far as I can see, it does not have any secret meaning at all. The bishop is

[46] Cyliani, *Hermes devoilé*. Paris, F. Locquin, 1832.

[47] H. de Lintaut, *L'Aurore*. Mss. Bibliothèque de l'Arsenal, S.A.F. 169, no. 3020.

[48] J-F. Henckel, *Traité de l'Appropriation*. Paris, Thomas Hérissant, 1760, p. 375, para. 416.

[49] *Explication de l'Enigme trouvé en un pilier de l'Eglise Nostre Dame de Paris* by the Sieur D.L.B. Paris, 1636.

standing on a finely hollowed out, oblong plinth, ornamented with
four little columns and an admirable Byzantine dragon, the whole
being supported by a pedestal bordered with a frieze and connected
to the base by a reversed ogee moulding. Only the plinth and the
pedestal have any hermetic value (pl. XXX).

Unfortunately this pillar, so magnificently decorated, is almost
new; it is scarcely sixty years since it was restored . . . and modified.
It is not my intention to discuss here the expediency of such repairs,
nor do I wish to imply that the leprosy of time should be allowed
to advance unchecked on a splendid body. All the same, as a
philosopher, I cannot but regret the careless attitude adopted by
restorers towards gothic creations. If it was thought fitting to replace
the blackened bishop and to restore his ruined base, such would be
an easy matter. It would suffice to copy the model, to transcribe it
faithfully. Even if it contained a hidden meaning, this would matter
little—servile imitation would have preserved it. But they wanted
to do better. On the one hand they did preserve the original lines of
the holy bishop and the fine dragon; but on the other hand they
ornamented the pedestal with foliage and Roman flourishes, in place
of the bezants and flowers which were there originally.

This second revised, corrected and augmented addition is certainly
richer than the first, but the symbolism is spoilt, the science is mutilated, the key lost, the esoteric meaning destroyed. Time corrodes,
wears away, decomposes and crumbles the limestone. The distinctness
of the outline suffers, but the sense remains. The restorer arrives,
the healer of stones; with a few strokes of the chisel he amputates,
cuts away, obliterates, transforms, makes an authentic ruin into an
artificial and brilliant anachronism. He makes wounds and dresses
them, takes away and overloads, prunes and counterfeits, all in the
name of Art, Form or Symmetry, without paying the least attention
to creative thought. Thanks to this modern cosmetic surgery, our
venerable ladies will always be young!

Alas! in meddling with the exterior, they have let the soul escape.

You disciples of Hermes, go to the cathedral and find out the
position and the order of the new pillar and then follow the track
of the original one. Cross the Seine, go into the Cluny museum and
you will have the satisfaction of finding it there, near the entrance

XXX.   NOTRE-DAME, PARIS.
(PORCH OF ST. ANNE—ST. MARCELLUS PILLAR)
Philosophic Mercury of the Great Work.

stairway in the frigidarium of the baths of Julian. It is there that the fine fragment has come to rest.[50]

On the right side of the cubic pedestal may be seen in relief two massive circular bezants. These are the metallic substances or *natures*—subject and solvent—with which one must begin the Work. On the principal face, these substances, modified by the preliminary operations, are no longer represented in the form of discs, but as roses with joined petals. In passing, one should unreservedly admire the skill of the artist in knowing how to translate the transformation of the occult products, freed from contingency and from the diverse materials which masked them before they were mined. On the left, the bezants, which have become roses, now take the form of decorative flowers with joined petals, but with the calyx showing. Although they are worn and almost effaced, it is easy to distinguish the trace of the central disc. They still represent the same subjects, now having acquired other qualities. The representation of the calyx shows that the mineral roots have been opened and are arranged to show their seminal principle. This is the estoric translation of the little motifs of the pedestal. The plinth will give us the complementary explanation.

[50] This itinerary is no longer valid. Six years ago the symbolical pillar being the object of much justified veneration, came back to Notre Dame and is now not far from the place which was its own for more than five hundred years. It is, in fact, to be found in a room with a high ceiling with surbased ribbed vaulting in the north tower, which is sooner or later to be arranged as a museum. An identical room may be found on the same floor, on the other side of the great organ platform.

In the meantime curiosity, of whatever kind, is not so easily satisfied, although it may drive the visitor all the way to this new refuge of initiatory sculpture. Alas! a surprise awaits him there, which will immediately sadden him. This consists in the most regrettable amputation of almost the whole body of the dragon, now reduced to the fore part only, but still retaining its two paws.

This monstrous beast, with the grace of some great lizard, used to embrace the athenor, leaving in its flames the triply-crowned little king, who is the son of its violent acts on the dead adultress. Only the face of the mineral child appears as it undergoes the 'baths of fire' mentioned by Nicholas Flamel. It is here swathed and tied up like the figure of the little 'bather', still found today in Epiphany cakes. (Cf. *Alchemie*, op. cit. p. 89.)

H

The matters, prepared and united in a single compound, must submit to sublimation or last purification by fire. In this operation the parts which can be burnt up are destroyed, the earthly matters lose their cohesion and disperse, while the pure, incombustible principles emerge in a higher form. This is the *Philosophers' Salt*, the king crowned with glory, who is born in the fire and must rejoice in the marriage which follows, in order, says Hermes, that hidden things may be made manifest. *Rex ab igne veniet, ac conjugio gaudebit et occulta patebunt.* The plinth shows us only the head of this king, emerging from the purifying flames. Today it is impossible to be sure that the frontal band engraved on the human head was once part of a crown. From the size and appearance of the skull, one could equally well take it for a sort of steel cap or helmet. Fortunately, however, we have the text of Esprit Gobineau de Montluisant, whose book was written on 'Wednesday, 20th May, 1640, the eve of the glorious Ascension of Our Saviour Jesus Christ',[51] and who tells us definitely that the king wears a *triple crown*.

After the raising of the pure and coloured principles of the philosophic compound, the residue is ready, from then on, to provide the volatile and fusible *mercurial salt*, to which the authors have often given the name *Babylonian Dragon*.

In creating this emblematic monster, the sculptor has produced a veritable chef-d'oeuvre and, although it is mutilated,—the left wing is broken—it remains none the less a remarkable piece of statuary. The fabulous beast emerges from the flames and its tail appears to come out of the human being, whose head it to some extent surrounds. Then, with a twisting movement which arches its back on the vaulting, it comes to grasp the athenor in its powerful claws.

If we examine the ornamentation of the plinth, we shall notice groups of shallow grooves, curved at the top and flat at the bottom. Those on the left face are accompanied by a flower with four unjoined petals. This expresses the universal matter, the quaternary of first elements according to the doctrine of Aristotle, which was cur-

---

[51] *Explication très curieuse des Enigmes et Figures hiéroglyphiques, Physiques, qui sont au grand portail de l'Eglise Cathedrale et Metropolitaine de Notre-Dame de Paris.*

rent in the Middle Ages. Directly below this is the duality of the two *natures*, on which the alchemist works and whose union provides the *Saturn(e)* of the Wise, this word being an anagram of *natures*. In the space between the columns of the front face there are four grooves of decreasing size, conforming to the slope of the flames above. These grooves symbolize the quaternary of *second elements*. Finally, on each side of the athenor and under the very claws of the dragon are the five unities of the *quintessence*, comprising the three principles and the two natures, and finally their total in the number ten 'in which everything finishes and comes to an end'.

L. P. Francois Cambriel[52] claims that the multiplication of the Sulphur—white or red—is not shown in the hieroglyph we are studying. I should not dare to make such a categorical assertion. The multiplication cannot in fact take place except by the aid of mercury, which plays the part of the patient in the Work, and by means of successive coctions or fixations. It is, therefore on the dragon, the sign of mercury, that we should look for the symbol representing the mutation and progression of the Sulphur or of the Elixir. Furthermore, if the author had taken more care in his examination of the decorative details, he would certainly have noticed:

1. A longitudinal band, beginning at the head and following the line of the backbone to the end of the tail.
2. Two similar bands, placed obliquely, one on each wing.
3. Two broader transverse bands round the tail of the dragon, the first at the level of the wing the other above the head of the king. All these bands are ornamented with full circles, touching at a point on their circumference.

As for the meaning, this will be supplied by the circles on the tail bands: the centre is very clearly marked on each one of them. Now, the hermeticists know that the king of the metals is symbolized by the solar sign, that is to say a circumference, with or without a central point. It therefore seems to me reasonable to think that if the dragon is covered with a profusion of auric symbols—it has them right down to the claws of the right paw—this is because it is capable of trans-

[52] L. P. Francois Cambriel, *Cours de Philosophie hermétique ou d'Alchimie en dix-neuf leçons*. Paris, Lacour et Maistrasse, 1843.

muting in quantity; but it can acquire this power only through a series of subsequent boiling operations with the *sulphur* or *philosophic gold*, which constitutes the *multiplications*.

This is the clearest possible statement of the esoteric meaning, which we thought we recognized on the excellent pillar of the St. Anne Portal. Others, more learned, will perhaps furnish a better interpretation of it, for I do not insist that anyone should accept the thesis developed here. Suffice it to say that it accords in general with the one given by Cambriel. But, on the other hand, I do not share the opinion of that author in wishing, without proof, to extend the symbolism of the plinth to the statue itself.

Truly, it is always painful to have to condemn an obvious mistake and even more distressing to point out certain statements in order to demolish them en bloc. However, this must be done, however much I may regret it. The science, which we are studying, is just as positive, as real and as exact as optics, geometry or mechanics; its results are as tangible as those of chemistry. In it, enthusiasm and private faith may act as stimulants and valuable helpers, but if they enter at all into the conduct and direction of our researches, we must not allow them to introduce any deviations. We must subordinate them to logic and reason and put them to the test of experience. Let us remember that it was the roguery of the greedy puffers, the senseless practices of the charlatans, the foolishness of ignorant and unscrupulous writers which brought discredit to the hermetic truth. One must have a right view and fitting speech. There must not be a word, which has not been weighed up, not a thought which has not been sifted by judgment and reflection. Alchemy asks to be purified; let us free it from the blemishes made on it, sometimes even by its own partisans. It will emerge all the stronger and healthier, without losing any of its charm or its mysterious attraction.

Francois Cambriel expresses himself in this way on the thirty-third page of his book: 'From this mercury results Life, represented by the bishop, who is above the said dragon. . . . The bishop *holds a finger to his mouth* in order to say to those who see him and who come to discover what he represents . . . "Be quiet! say nothing about this. . . ." '

The text is accompanied by an engraved plate, very badly drawn—

not that that matters much—but notoriously faked—which is more serious. In it, St. Marcellus holds a crozier, as short as a gate-keeper's flag. On his head is a mitre, decorated with a cross, and, as a superb anachronism, this pupil of Prudence is wearing a beard! A piquant detail is that the dragon in the opposite picture is shown with his jaws sideways on, gnawing the foot of the poor bishop, who, however, appears to worry very little about this. Calm and smiling, he is engaged in closing his lips with his right forefinger in a gesture of enjoining silence.

It is easy to verify this, since we possess the original work, and the fraud strikes us at the first glance. Our saint, in accordance with the medieval custom, is completely clean-shaven. His very simple mitre has no ornamentation at all. The bottom of his crozier, which he supports with his left hand, is resting on the jaws of the dragon. As for the famous gesture, made by the characters in the *Mutus Liber* and by Harpocrates, it is here entirely a figment of Cambriel's excessive imagination. St. Marcellus is shown giving the blessing, in an attitude full of nobility, his head bowed, his forearm bent upwards, his hand on a level with his shoulder, the first and middle fingers raised.

It is difficult to believe that two observers could have been the dupes of the same illusion. Does this fantasy come from the artist or was it imposed by the text? The description and the drawing are so much in accord that I must be forgiven for giving very little credence to the powers of observation shown in this other fragment by the same author.

'Passing one day in front of the church of Notre Dame of Paris, I examined *with great attention* the fine sculptures, ornamenting the three doors, and I saw on one of these doors one of the most beautiful hieroglyphs I have ever seen. *For several days on end, I went to look at it*, in order to be able to give details of all it represented, and this I managed. The reader will be convinced of this by what follows, or, better still, *by betaking himself to the spot.*'

Surely neither boldness nor impudence are lacking here. If Cambriel's reader accepts his invitation, he will find nothing on the pier of the St. Anne door but the exoteric legend of St. Marcellus. He will see there the bishop killing the dragon by touching it with his crozier, as is reported by tradition. The idea that he also symbolizes the life of matter is a personal opinion of the author, which he is free to express; but that he is representing the Zoroastrian injunction to keep silence is not, and never was, the case.

Such folly is regrettable and unworthy of a sincere, honest and upright spirit.

7

Our great cathedrals, built by medieval *Freemasons* in order to ensure the transmission of hermetic symbols and doctrine, have from the time of their appearance exercised a marked influence on numerous more modest examples of civil or religious architecture.

Flamel took pleasure in covering the many buildings, which he erected, with hieroglyphs and emblems. The Abbé Villain tells us that the little portal of St. Jacques-la-Boucherie, which the Adept commissioned in 1389, was covered in figures. 'On the west post of the portal,' he says 'a little sculptured angel is seen, holding a circle of stone in his hands; Flamel had a circular piece of black marble incorporated in it, with a thread of fine gold in the form of a cross. . . .'[53] The poor had his generosity to thank also for two houses, which he had built in the Rue du Cimitière-de-St. Nicolas-des-Champs, the first in 1407 and the other in 1410. 'These buildings showed,' Salmon informs us, 'a quantity of figures engraved on the stones, with a gothic N and F on either side'. The chapel of the Hôpital St. Gervais, rebuilt at his expense, was in no way inferior to the other foundations. 'The façade and the portal of the new chapel,' writes Albert Poisson,[54] 'were covered with figures and legends in Flamel's usual manner.' The portal of St. Geneviève-des-Ardents, situated in the Rue de la Tixanderie, preserved its interesting symbolism until the middle of the eighteenth century, at which time the church was converted into a house and the ornaments on the façade were destroyed. Flamel also erected two decorative arcades

[53] Abbé Villain, *Histoire critique de Nicolas Flamel*. Paris, Desprez, 1761.

[54] Albert Poisson, *Histoire de l'Alchimie. Nicolas Flamel*. Paris, Chacornac, 1893.

in the Charnier des Innocents, one in 1389 and the second in 1407. Poisson tells us that the first showed, among other hieroglyphic plaques, a coat of arms, which the Adept 'seems to have copied from another one, attributed to St. Thomas Aquinas'. The celebrated occultist adds that it appears at the end of Lagneau's *Harmonie Chymique*. At any rate, this is the description which he gives of it:

'The coat of arms is divided into four by a cross. The latter has in the middle a crown of thorns, enclosing in its centre a bleeding heart, from which rises a reed. In one of the quarters one sees IEVE, written in Hebrew characters, in the midst of a host of luminous rays and below a black cloud. In the second quarter there is a crown. In the third, the earth bears a rich harvest and the fourth is occupied by the spheres of fire.'

This account, which is in accordance with Lagneau's engraving, allows us to conclude that the latter had his picture copied from the arcade of the cemetery. There is nothing impossible in this, since three of the four plaques still remained at the time of Gohorry, i.e. about 1572—and the *Harmonie Chymique* was brought out by Claude Morel in 1601. However, it would have been preferable to refer to the original coat of arms, which was rather different from Flamel's and much less obscure. It was still extant at the time of the Revolution, on a stained glass window, lighting the chapel of St. Thomas Aquinas at the Convent of the Jacobins. This church of the Dominicans—who lived there and had established themselves about the year 1217—owed its foundation to Louis IX. It was situated in the Rue St. Jacques and dedicated to St. James the Great. The *Curiositez de Paris*, which was published in 1716 by Saugrain the elder, adds that the schools of the Angelic Doctor were situated beside the church.

This coat of arms, said to be that of St. Thomas Aquinas, was drawn and painted very accurately in 1787 from the window itself by a hermeticist named Chaudet. It is this drawing which enables me to give a description of it (pl. XXXI).

The quartered French shield is surmounted by a rounded segment. This supplementary piece shows a reversed matrass[55] or, surrounded

---

[55]*Translator's note:* a matrass is a round glass vessel with a neck, used for distilling.

by a crown of thorns vert on a field sable. A cross or bears three roundels azure at base and arms dexter and sinister and has a heart gules at the centre with a branch vert. Tears argent, falling from the matrass, are collected and fixed on this heart. The dexter chief quarter, halved or three stars purpure and azure seven rays or, is opposite sinister base a ground sable with ears of corn or on a field tenné. In the sinister chief quarter a cloud violet on a field argent and three arrows of the same, feathered or, pointing towards the abyss. Dexter base three serpents argent on a field vert.

This fine emblem has all the more importance for us, because it unveils the secrets relating to the extraction of mercury and its conjunction with sulphur. These are obscure points in the practice, on which all the authors have preferred to maintain a religious silence.

Pierre de Montereau's masterpiece, the Sainte Chapelle, that marvellous stone shrine, erected between 1245 and 1248 to house the relics of the Passion, also presented a most remarkable alchemical ensemble. Even today, although we may strongly regret the restoration of the original portal, where the Parisians of 1830 could, with Victor Hugo, admire 'two angels, one with his hand in a vase and the other in a cloud', we still have the joy of possessing intact the southern stained glass windows of this splendid building. It would be difficult to firrd anywhere a more considerable collection based on esoteric principles than that of the Sainte Chapelle. It would be too enormous a task, and one which could provide the subject matter of many volumes, to undertake, leaf by leaf, the description of such a veritable forest of glass. I will, therefore, limit myself to giving a specimen extract from the first mullion of the fifth bay, which refers to the Massacre of the Innocents, the meaning of which I have already given. I cannot too highly commend to lovers of our ancient science, as well as to those desirous of learning about the occult, the study of the symbolic windows of the high chapel. They will find an enormous amount of information to be gleaned there, as well as in the great rose window, that incomparable creation of colour and harmony.

XXXI.   SYMBOLIC COAT OF ARMS (XIIIth CENTURY)

XXXII.   SAINTE-CHAPELLE, PARIS—
SOUTHERN STAINED GLASS WINDOWS
The Massacre of the Innocents.

Amiens

Amiens, like Paris, presents a remarkable collection of hermetic bas-reliefs. A strange fact, and one which is worth noting, is that the central porch of Notre Dame of Amiens—the Porch of the Saviour—is a more or less faithful reproduction, not only of the motifs adorning the portal of Paris, but even of the order in which they are given. In Paris the figures hold discs, while here it is shields; the emblem of mercury is displayed by a woman at Amiens and by a man in Paris. There are the same symbols on the two buildings, the same attributes. Actions and costumes are similar. There can be no doubt that the work of Guillaume of Paris exercised a considerable influence on the decoration of the great porch at Amiens.

At any rate, this most magnificent masterpiece of Picardy remains one of the purest documents bequeathed to us by the Middle Ages. What is more, its state of preservation made it possible for the restorers to respect the great part of the subjects; thus, this splendid temple, which owes its origin to the genius of Robert de Luzarches and Thomas and Renault de Cormont, remains today in its original glory.

Among the allegories characteristic of the style of Amiens, I would first mention the ingenious interpretation of the *fire of the wheel*. The philosopher, who is seated with his elbow resting on his right knee, appears to be meditating or keeping watch (pl. XXXIII).

This quatrefoil, which from our point of view is very characteristic, has, however, received an entirely different interpretation from some authors. Jourdain and Duval, Ruskin *(The Bible of Amiens)*, the Abbé Roze and, after them, Georges Durand[1] have found the meaning of it in the prophecy of Ezekiel, who, says Durand, 'saw four winged beasts, as St. John was to do later, and then some wheels, one within the other. It is the vision of the wheels which is represented here. Naively taking the words literally, the artist has reduced the vision to its simplest expression. The prophet is seated on a rock and seems to be sleeping, leaning on his right knee. In front of him appear two cart wheels and that is all.'

This version contains two errors. The first shows an incomplete study of the traditional techniques, of the formulas respected by the *latomi* in the execution of their symbols. The second, a graver one, results from defective observation.

In reality, our imagers were accustomed to separate, or at least to underline, their supernatural attributes with a bank of clouds. An example of this may be seen on the face of the three piers of the porch, but there is nothing of that here. Moreover, our character has his eyes open, so he is not asleep, but appears to be keeping watch, while the slow action of the *fire of the wheel* takes place close to him. Further, it is well known that in gothic scenes illustrating visions, the illuminate is always shown facing the phenomenon;

[1] G. Durand, *Monographie de l'Eglise cathedrale d'Amiens*. Paris, A. Picard, 1901.

XXXIII.   AMIENS CATHEDRAL—PORCH OF THE SAVIOUR
The Fire of the Wheel.

his attitude and his expression invariably bearing witness to surprise or ecstasy, anxiety or bliss. This is not the case in the subject in hand. The wheels are, then, and can only be, an image, whose meaning is hidden from the profane, and which is put into the picture in order to veil something as well known to the initiate as to the character himself. Moreover, he is not at all absorbed in any pre-occupation of this kind. He is awake and keeps watch, patiently, but a little languidly. The hard *labours of Hercules* are accomplished and his work has been reduced to the *ludus puerorum* (child's play) of the texts, i.e. to keeping up the fire, which can easily be under-taken and carried out successfully by a woman spinning with a distaff.

As for the double image of the hieroglyph, we must interpret it as the sign of the two revolutions, which must act in succession on the compound in order to ensure for it the first degree of perfection. Unless one prefers to see in it an indication of the two natures in the *conversion*, which is also achieved by means of gentle and regular heating. This latter thesis is adopted by Pernety.

Actually, *linear and continuous* coction demands the *double rotation* of one and the same wheel, which is a movement impossible to convey in stone and which justifies the necessity of having two wheels overlapping in such a way as to form only one. The first wheel corresponds to the *humid phase* of the operation—called *elixation*—in which the compound remains melted until a light film is formed. This, as it gradually becomes thicker, gains in depth. The second period, characterized by dryness—or *assation*—then begins with a second turn of the wheel and is completed and perfected when the contents of the *egg*, which has been calcined, appears granulated or powdery, in the form of crystals, sand or ashes.

The anonymous commentator of a classic work[2] says concerning this operation, which is veritably the seal of the Great Work, that 'the philosopher boils with gentle solar heat in a single vessel a single vapour, which thickens little by little'. But what can be the temperature of the external fire, suitable for this coction? Accord-

---

[2] *La Lumière sortant par soy-mesme des Ténèbres*, Paris, d'Houry, 1687, ch. III, p. 30.

ing to modern authors, the temperature at the beginning should not exceed the heat of the human body. Albert Poisson gives 50° as a basis, increasing progressively up to around 300° Centigrade. Phila-lethes, in his *Rules*,[3] affirms that 'that degree of heat which could hold the lead (327°) or tin (232°) in fusion, or even greater, that is to say such that the vessels could bear it without breaking, must be called a *temperate heat*. 'With that,' he says, 'you will begin your degree of heat proper to the realm in which nature has placed you.' In his fifteenth rule, Philalethes reverts to this important question. After having stressed that the artist must operate on the mineral bodies and not on the organic substances, he speaks thus:

'It is necessary that the water of our lake should boil with the ashes of the tree of Hermes; I exhort you to boil it night and day without ceasing, in order that, in the movements of our tempestuous sea, the celestial nature may rise and the terrestial sink. For I assure you that if we do not boil it, we can never call our work a *coction*, but a *digestion*.'

Beside the *fire of the wheel* I would point out a small subject sculptured on the right of the same porch and which G. Durand takes to be a replica of the seventh medallion of Paris. This is what the author says about it (bk. I, p. 336):

'M. Jourdain and M. Duval had given the name Inconstancy to the vice which is the opposite of Perseverance, but it seems to me that the word Apostasy, suggested by the Abbé Roze, is more apt for the subject represented. It is a bare-headed figure, clean-shaven and tonsured, a clerk or a monk, wearing a calf-length tunic with a hood, differing from the dress of the clerk, in the group illustrating Anger, only in being drawn in by a belt. Throwing aside his hose and his footwear, a sort of half boots, he seems to be leaving a pretty little church with long, narrow windows, a cylindrical belfry and a sham door, shown in the background (pl. XXXIV).' In a footnote, Durand adds: 'On the great portal of Notre Dame in Paris, the apostate leaves his garments in the church itself; on the stained glass window of the same church, he is shown on the outside, making the gesture

[3] *Règles de Philalèthe pour se conduire dans l'Oeuvre hermétique*, in *Histoire de la Philosophie hermétique*, by Lenglet-Dufresnoy, Paris, Coustelier, 1742, bk. II.

XXXIV.   AMIENS CATHEDRAL—PORCH OF THE SAVIOUR
Philosophic Coction.

XXXV.   AMIENS CATHEDRAL—CENTRAL PORCH
The Cock and the Fox.

of a man who is running away. At Chartres, he has undressed almost completely, wearing nothing but his shirt. Ruskin remarks that the unbelieving fool is always represented barefoot in the miniatures of the twelfth and thirteenth centuries.'

For my part, I find no correspondence between the motif of Paris and the one at Amiens. Whereas the former symbolizes the beginning of the Work, the latter, on the contrary, interprets its end. The church is, rather, an athenor and its belfry erected, without regard to the most elementary rules of architecture, is the secret furnace, enclosing the philosophic egg. This furnace is provided with openings, through which the craftsman watches the phases of the work. One important and very characteristic detail has been forgotten. I am speaking of the hollowed out arch at the base. Now, it is difficult to admit that a church could be built on visible vaults and thus appear to rest on four feet. It is no less rash to take as a garment the limp mass, to which the artist is pointing with his finger. These considerations have led me to believe that the motif at Amiens is concerned with hermetic symbolism and represents the coction itself, as well as its apparatus. The alchemist is pointing with his right hand to the coal sack and the fact that he has abandoned his footwear is sufficient indication of the extent to which prudence and the concern for silence must be carried in this secret task. As for the light clothing worn by the craftsman in the motif at Chartres, this is justified by the heat given off by the furnace. At the fourth degree of fire, when proceeding by the dry method, it becomes necessary to maintain a temperature of close on 1200°, which is also indispensable in projection. Our modern workers in the metallurgical industry dress in the same scant way as the puffer of Chartres. I should certainly be glad to know the reason why apostates feel it necessary to doff their clothes when leaving the temple. It is just this reason which should have been given in order to uphold and support the thesis propounded by the above-mentioned authors.

We have seen how, at Notre Dame of Paris, the athenor takes precisely this form of a tower raised on arches. It is self apparent that it could not have been reproduced esoterically exactly as it existed in the laboratory. Therefore they confined themselves to giving it an architectural form, without, however, losing those characteristics which could reveal its true intention. The constituent parts of the alchemical furnace may be recognized in it; the ash box, the tower and the dome. Moreover, those who have consulted the old engravings—and particularly the woodcuts of *Pyrotechny*, which Jean Liébaut inserted in his treatise[4]—will not make any mistake about it. The furnaces are shown as castle keeps, with their sloping banks, their battlements and their loopholes. Certain combinations of these apparatuses go so far as to assume the appearance of buildings or little fortresses, from which the spouts of their alembics and the necks of their retorts protrude.

Against the bottom of the right hand side of the great porch, we shall find in an engaged quatrefoil the allegory of the *cock* and the *fox*, dear to Basil Valentine. The cock is perched on an *oak* branch, which the fox is trying to reach (pl. XXXV). The uninitiated will see in this the subject of a fable, popular in the Middle Ages, which, according to Jourdain and Duval, is the prototype of the crow and the fox. 'The dogs, which complete the fable, are not shown here,' adds G. Durand. This typical detail does not seem to have drawn the attention of the authors to the occult meaning of the symbol. Yet our ancestors, who were exact and meticulous interpreters, would not have failed to portray these characters, if it had been a question of a well-known scene from a fable.

For the benefit of our brothers, the sons of science, it would perhaps not be out of place here to go a little more fully into the meaning of this image than I thought necessary to do in the case of the same emblem, sculptured on the porch in Paris. I shall doubtless explain later the close connection existing between the *cock* and the *oak*, which would find an analogy in family relationships; for the son is united to his father as the cock is to his tree. For the moment, I will just say that the *cock* and the *fox* are no more than the same hierolglyph covering two distinct physical states of one and the same matter. What appears first is the *cock*, or the *volatile* part, which is consequently alive, active, full of movement, extracted from the subject, which has the oak tree for its emblem. Here again is our famous spring, whose clear water flows at the base of the sacred tree,

[4] Cf. Jean Liébaut, *Quatre Livres des Secrets de Medicine et de la Philosophie Chimique*. Paris, Jacques du Puys, 1579, p. 17a and 19a.

which the Druids so much venerated. This spring the ancient philosophers called Mercury, although it has none of the appearance of
common quicksilver. The water we need is *dry*, it does not wet the
hands and it gushes out of the rock at a blow from Aaron's rod. That
is the alchemical meaning of the *cock*, the emblem of *Mercury* to the
pagan and of the *resurrection* to the Christian. This *cock*, volatile
though it may be, can become the *Phoenix*. It must first of all assume
that state of provisional fixity, characterized by the symbol of our
hermetic *fox*. Before undertaking the practice, it is important to
know that the *mercury* contains in itself *everything necessary for the
work*. 'Blessed be the All-Highest,' cries Geber, 'who has created this
Mercury and given it a nature, which nothing can resist! For without it the alchemists would have worked in vain, all their labour
would have been useless.' It is the only matter, which we need. Indeed, although this *dry water* is entirely volatile, if one can find the
means of keeping it on the fire for a long time it is capable of becoming sufficiently fixed to resist that degree of heat which would
otherwise have been sufficient to evaporate it totally. These new
properties, the heavy quality and the ability to resist fire, entitle it to
a new emblem and the fox is used to symbolize this new nature. *The
water has become earth* and the mercury sulphur. However, this
earth, in spite of the fine colouration which it has taken on during
its long contact with the fire, would not be any good in its dry form.
An old saying tells us that *all dry colouring is useless in its dryness*.
It is, therefore, expedient to dissolve this earth or this salt again in
the same water which gave it birth, or—which amounts to the same
thing—*in its own blood*. In this way it may become volatile a second
time and the *fox* may reassume the complexion, the wings and the
tail of the *cock*. By a second operation, similar to the first, the compound will coagulate again. It will struggle again against the tyranny
of the fire, but this time in the fusion itself and no longer because
of its dry quality. Thus the first stone will be born, being neither
absolutely fixed nor absolutely volatile, but permanent enough on
the fire, very penetrating and very fusible. You will have to increase
these qualities by means of a *third repetition* of the same technique.
Then the *cock*, the attribute of St. Peter, the true and fluid stone on
which the whole Christian edifice rests, *will have crowed thrice.*

I

For it is he, the first apostle, who holds the two *crossed keys* of solution and coagulation. It is he, who is the symbol of the volatile stone, which the fire renders fixed and dense as it is precipitated. Let no one forget that St. Peter was crucified *head downwards.* . . .

Among the fine motifs of the north portal, or the Portal of St. Firmin, which is almost entirely taken up with the zodiac and rural or domestic scenes corresponding to it, I would point out two interesting bas-reliefs. The first represents a citadel, whose massive bolted door is flanked by crenellated towers, between which rise two levels of construction, the basement being ornamented with a grille. Is this the symbol of philosophical, social, moral and religious esotericism, which is revealed and developed right through the hundred and fifteen other quatrefoils? Or should we see in this motif of the year 1225 the original idea of the *alchemical fortress*, which was taken up, adopted and modified by Khunrath in 1609? Should it rather be the mysterious closed *palace* of the King of our Art, mentioned by Basil Valentine and Philalethes? Whatever it may be, citadel or royal residence, the building, with its imposing and grim appearance, produces a real impression of strength and impregnability. It seems to have been built to preserve some treasure or to conceal some important secret and no one can enter there, unless he possesses thet kay to the powerful locks, which protect it against all attempts to break in. It is like a prison or a cave and the door suggests something sinister, full of dread, which makes you think of the entrance to Tartarus;

Abandon hope, all ye who enter here.

The second quatrefoil, placed immediately below the first, shows some dead trees, twisting and interlacing their knotty branches beneath a sky, which has been partially defaced, but in which the images of the sun, the moon and some stars may still be discerned (pl. XXXVI).

This subject refers to the first matter of the great Art, the metallic planets, whose death, the Philosophers tell us, has been caused by the fire, and which have been rendered by the fusion inert and without vegetative power, as the trees are in winter.

This is why the Masters have so often advised us to *reincrude* them by providing them, in their fluid form, with the *proper agent*, which they lost in the metallurgical reduction. But where can this agent be found? This is the great mystery, on which I have frequently touched in the course of this study, by dividing it up piecemeal into emblems, so that only the discerning investigator will be able to recognize its qualities and identify the substance. I did not want to follow the ancient method of giving a truth, expressed in a parable, accompanied by one or many specious or captious allegations, in order to lead astray the reader who is incapable of separating the chaff from the wheat. Most certainly, one can discuss and critize this work, which is more unrewarding than can be imagined; I do not think that I shall ever be reproached for having written a single lie. We are assured that not every truth may be told; I think that, despite the proverb, it is possible to make it understood by using some subtlety of language. 'Our Art,' as Artephius once said, 'is entirely cabalistic'. Indeed, the cabala has always been of great use to me. It has allowed me, without distorting the truth, without perverting the means of expression, falsifying science or perjuring myself, to say many things, which I have sought in vain in the books of my predecessors. Sometimes, faced with the impossibility of going further without breaking my vow, I have preferred to keep silent rather than to make deceptive allusions or abuse a confidence.

What am I to say, when faced here with the *Secret of Secrets*, with this *Verbum dimissum* which I have already mentioned and which Jesus confided to his Apostles, as St. Paul testifies: [5]

'Whereof I am made a minister, according to the dispensation of God, which is given to me for you, to fulfil the word of God; even the mystery *which hath been hid from ages and from generations*, but now is made manifest to his saints.'

What can I say, except to quote the testimony of the great masters, who have themselves sought to explain it?

'Metallic chaos, a product of the hands of nature, contains in itself all metals and is not metal. It contains gold, silver and mercury; but it is neither gold, nor silver, nor mercury.'[6] This text is clear. If you

[5] *Epistle to the Colossians*, ch. I, v. 25 and 26.
[6] *Le Psautier d'Hermophile* in *Traités des Metaux*. Mss. anon. of eighteenth century, strophe XXV.

prefer symbolical language, Haymon[7] gives an example of this, when he says:

'In order to obtain the first agent, you must go to the uttermost part of the *world*, when you hear the thunder growling, the wind blowing, the hail and rain falling; it is there that you will find the thing, if you seek it.'

All the descriptions left us by the Philosophers about this subject, or first matter, which contains the essential agent, are extremely confused and very mysterious. Here are some, chosen from among the best.

The author of the commentary on *La Lumière sortant des Tènebres* writes on p. 108: 'The essence in which the spirit we are seeking dwells is grafted and engraved on it, although with imperfect lines and lineaments. The same thing is said by Ripley at the beginning of his *Twelve Gates*; and Aegidius de Vadis in his *Dialogue de la Nature* shows clearly, as though written in letters of gold, that a portion of this *first chaos* has remained in this *world*, which is known but despised by everyone and is sold publicly.' The same author also says on p. 263 that 'this *subject* is found in various places and in each of the three kingdoms; but if we look to nature's possibilities it is certain that the sole *metallic nature* must be aided from and by nature; it is, thus, only in the *mineral* kingdom, where the metallic seed dwells, that we must seek the subject proper to our art.'

'It is a stone of great virtue,' says Nicholas Valois[8] in his turn, 'and is called stone, but is not stone and is mineral, vegetable and animal, which is found in every place and at every time and with every person.'

Flamel[9] writes similarly: 'There is an occult stone, concealed and buried in the depths of a fountain, which is vile, abject and valued not at all; it is also covered with filth and excrement; to which all names are given, although there is really only one. This stone, says

[7] Haymon, *Epistola de Lapidibus Philosophicis*. Treatise 192, bk. VI of *Theatrum Chemicum*. Argentorati, 1613.

[8] *Oeuvres de N, Grosparmy et Nicolas Valois*, ms. quoted supra, p. 140.

[9] Nicholas Flamel, *Original du Désiré*, or *Thrésor de Philosophie*. Paris, Hulpeau, 1629, p. 144.

XXXVI.   AMIENS CATHEDRAL—PORCH OF ST. FIRMIN
The first Matters.

XXXVII.   AMIENS CATHEDRAL—
PORCH OF THE VIRGIN MOTHER
The Philosophers' Dew.

Morien the Wise, which is not a stone, is animated, having the virtue of procreating and engendering. This stone is soft, owing its beginning, origin and race to Saturn or to Mars, the Sun and Venus; and if it is Mars, the Sun and Venus. . . .'

'There is,' says le Breton,[10] 'a mineral known to the truly Wise, concealed by them under various names in their writings, which contains abundantly both the fixed and the volatile.'

'The Philosophers were right,' writes an anonymous author,[11] 'to hide this mystery from the eyes of those who value things only by the usages they have given them; for if they knew, or if they were openly shown the Matter, which God has been pleased to hide in things which appear to them useful, they would no longer value them.' This is a similar idea to the one expressed in the *Imitation*[12] p. 170, which is the last of these abstruse quotations which I shall give: 'He, who esteems things according to their value and not according to the merit or esteem of men, possesses true Wisdom.'

Let us return to the façade at Amiens. The anonymous master, who sculptured the medallions in the Porch of the Virgin Mother, has given a very curious interpretation to the condensation of the universal spirit. An adept is contemplating the stream of *celestial dew* falling on a mass, which a number of authors have taken for a fleece. Without condemning this opinion, it is equally plausible to suspect here a different body, such as that mineral designated by the name of *Magnesia* or *philosophic lodestone*. It will be noticed that this water does not fall on anything else but the subject under consideration, which suggests the presence of an attracting quality hidden in this body. That it is important to try to identify (pl. XXXVII).

This is, I believe, the place to rectify certain errors which have been made concerning a symbolical vegetable matter, which, when taken literally by ignorant puffers, has largely been responsible for bringing discredit on alchemy and ridicule on its adherents. I mean

[10] Le Breton, *Clefs de la Philosophie Spagyrique*. Paris, Jombert, 1722, p. 240.
[11] *La Clef du Cabinet hermétique*, ms. quoted supra, p. 10.
[12] *The Imitation of Christ*, bk. II, ch. 1, v. 6.

Nostoc. This cryptogam,[13] which rural people well know, is found all over the country, sometimes on the grass, sometimes on the bare earth, in fields, beside paths, on the edge of woods. In the early morning in spring, you will find masses of it, swollen with the morning dew. These plants, which are jelly-like and trembling—hence the French name *Trémelles*—are usually greenish and dry up so rapidly under the action of the sun's rays that it is impossible to find any trace of them, even on the spot where they had opened out only a few hours previously. The combination of all these characteristics— sudden appearance, absorption of water and swelling, green colour, soft and glutinous consistency—have prompted the philosophers to take these algae as the hieroglyph of their matter. Now, it is most certainly a mass of this sort, symbolizing the mineral *Magnesia* of the Wise, which is seen in the quatrefoil at Amiens, absorbing the celestial dew. I will quickly run through the many names given to the Nostoc, which, to the Masters, indicated their mineral principle: *Celestial fundament Moon-Spit, Earth-Butter, Dew-Grease, Vegetable Vitriol, Flos Caeli* (heavenly flower), etc. according to whether they regarded it as a receptacle of the universal Spirit, or as a terrestial matter exhaled from the centre in a state of vapour, then coagulated by cooling in contact with the air.

These strange terms, which have, however, their justification, have caused the real and initiatory significance of the *Nostoc* to be forgotten. This word comes from the Greek νυξ, νυκτος corresponding to the Latin *nox, noctis*, night. Thus it is something which is *born at night*, which needs the night in order to develop and can work only at night. Thus *our subject* is admirably concealed from profane eyes, although it could easily be distinguished and uncovered by those possessing exact knowledge of natural laws. But, alas! how few take the trouble to reflect and how few retain simplicity of reasoning.

Look here, we say, you who have *laboured* so hard, what are you claiming to do with your lighted furnaces, your many, varied and useless utensils? Do you hope to accomplish a veritable *creation* out of all the pieces? Certainly not, since the faculty of creation be-

[13] *Translator's note:* cryptogam—a plant having no stamens or pistil and therefore no proper flowers.

longs only to God, the one Creator. Then it must be a generative process which you hope to bring about within your materials. But in that case you must have the help of nature and you may be sure that this help will be refused to you, if, by ill fortune or from ignorance, you do not put nature in a position where its laws can be applied. What, then, is this *primordial condition*, which is essential if any generation is to take place? I will reply on your behalf: *the total absence of any solar light*, even when diffused or filtered. Look around you, consult your own nature. Do you not see that with man and with animals *fecundation* and *generation* take place, thanks to a certain disposition of organs, in *complete obscurity*, maintained until the time of birth? Is it on the surface of the earth—in full light—or within the earth itself—in darkness—that vegetable seeds can germinate and be reproduced? Is it during the day or the night that the life-giving dew falls, which feeds and vitalizes them? Take the mushroom, is it not during the night that it grows and develops? And as for you yourself, is it not also during the night, in sleep, that your organism repairs its losses, eliminates its waste matter, builds new cells, new tissue, in place of those burnt up and destroyed by daylight? There is no process, even down to the work of digestion, the assimilation of food and its transformation into blood and organic substance, which does not take place in the dark. Would you like to try an experiment? Take some fertile eggs and hatch them in a well-lighted room. At the end of the incubation, all your eggs will contain dead embryos, more or less in a state of decomposition. Any chick that is born is blind, sickly and will not survive. That is the fatal effect of the sun, not on the vitality of established individuals, but on the generative process. Do not think either that these effects of a fundamental law of nature are limited to the *organic* kingdoms. Even minerals, in spite of their less obvious reaction, are subject to it, as well as animals and vegetables. It is well known that the production of a photographic image is based on the property, possessed by the salts of silver, of *decomposing* in light. These salts resume their inert, metallic state, whereas in the dark room they had acquired an active, living and sensitive quality. When two gases, chlorine and hydrogen, are mixed, each preserves its own integrity as long as darkness is maintained; they combine slowly in a diffused light and with a violent explosion in sunlight. A large number of metallic salts in solution are transformed or precipitated more or less rapidly in daylight. Thus ferrous sulphate is rapidly changed into ferric sulphate.

It is, therefore, important to remember that the sun is the destroyer par excellence of all substances too young and too feeble to resist its fiery power. This is so much a fact that a therapeutic method of curing external ailments has been based on its special action. This method is the rapid cicatrisation of sores and wounds. The deadly power of the sun, firstly on microbes and then on organic cells has made possible the institution of phototherapy.

And now, work in the daylight if you like, but do not blame me if your efforts never lead to success. I know, myself, that the goddess Isis is the mother of all things, that she bears them all in her womb and that she alone can bestow *Revelation* and *Initiation*. You unbelievers, who have eyes that you may not see and ears that you may not hear, to whom do you address your prayers? Do you not know that you can reach Jesus only through the intercession of *his Mother; Sancta Maria, ora pro nobis?* And, for your instruction, the Virgin is represented with her feet resting on the *lunar* crescent and always dressed in blue, the symbolic colour of the night star. I could say much more, but I think I have spoken enough.

Let us, then, end this study of the original hermetic types of Amiens Cathedral by pointing out a little corner motif to the left of the same Porch of the Virgin Mother, which shows an initiation scene. The Master is indicating to three of his disciples the *hermetic star*, about which I have already spoken at length. This is the traditional star, which acts as guide to the Philosophers and shows them the birth of *the son of the sun* (pl. XXXVIII). In connection with this star, let us recall the emblem of Nicholas Rollin, Chancellor to Philip the Good, painted in 1447 on the floor of the hospital at Beaune, which he founded. This emblem, given in the form of a riddle: 'Only ✷ indicated the science of its owner by this characteristic *sign* of the Work, the one and *only star*.

XXXVIII.   AMIENS CATHEDRAL—
PORCH OF THE VIRGIN MOTHER
The seven-rayed Star.

Bourges

1

Bourges, that ancient city of the Province of Berri, is silent, withdrawn, calm and grey like a monastery cloister. As well as being justly proud of its fine cathedral, it has other equally remarkable buildings to offer to lovers of the past, the purest jewels in its magnificent crown being the great house of Jacques Coeur and the Lallement mansion.

I shall not say much about the first, which was formerly a veritable museum of hermetic emblems. Successive waves of vandalism have swept over it, ruining the interior decoration. Faced with those empty walls, those dilapidated rooms, those high, vaulted galleries, now out of commission, it would be quite impossible to imagine the

original magnificence of this palatial house, were it not for the fact
that the façade has been preserved in its original state.

Jacques Coeur, the great silversmith of the reign of Charles VII,
had the reputation of being a proven adept. Indeed David de Planis-
Campy mentions him as possessing 'the precious gift of the white
stone', in other words the power of transmuting common metals into
silver. Hence, perhaps, his title of silversmith. Be that as it may, we
must recognize that Jacques Coeur, using a profusion of symbols
of his own choosing, did all he could to validate his real or supposed
status as a *philosopher by fire*.

Everyone knows the coat of arms and the device of this promin-
ent personage: three hearts forming the centre of the following inscription, given in the form of a riddle: *A vaillans cuer riens impossible* (To the valiant heart nothing is impossible). This proud motto,
bursting with energy, takes on a rather singular meaning if we examine it according to cabalistic rules. Indeed, if we read *cuer* with the
spelling of the period, we shall obtain at the same time:

1. The statement of the universal Spirit *(ray of light)*.
2. The common name for the basic matter, which has been pro-
   cessed (the *iron*).
3. The three repetitions essential for the complete perfection of
   the two Magisteries *(the three hearts)*.

It is, therefore, my conviction that Jacques Coeur practised alchemy
himself, or at least that he saw before his very eyes the develop-
ment of the white stone, which had been 'essencified' by the iron
and boiled three times.

Among our silversmith's favourite hieroglyphs, the heart and the
scallop shell hold pride of place. These two images are always
coupled together or placed symmetrically. This may be seen on the
central motifs of the quadrilobate circles on the windows, on the
balustrades, on the panels and on the door knocker, etc. No doubt
this duality of the shell and the heart contains a pun on the name of
the owner or his shorthand signature. However, shells of the comb
genus (Pecten Jacobaeus to the naturalists) have always been used
as the badge of St. James' pilgrims. They were worn either on the
hat (as we see in a statue of St. James in Westminster Abbey) or

XXXIX.   JACQUES COEUR'S HOUSE—FAÇADE
The Scallop Shell.

XL.   JACQUES COEUR'S HOUSE—TREASURE CHAMBER
Tristan and Isolde Group.

round the neck, or else fastened on the chest, always in a very obvious manner. The *shell of Compostella* (pl. XXXIX), about which I shall have a good deal to say, is used in secret symbolism to stand for the principle of Mercury,[1] which is still called the *Traveller* or the *Pilgrim*. It is worn mystically by all those who undertake the work and seek to obtain the star *(compos stella)*. It is, therefore, not surprising that Jacques Coeur should have had a reproduction of this *icon peregrini,* so popular with medieval puffers, placed at the entrance to his mansion. Does Nicholas Flamel not describe in the same way, in his *Figures Hiéroglyphiques,* the symbolic journey which he undertook in order, as he says, to ask 'Monsieur James of Galicia' for help, light and protection. This is where all alchemists must begin. With the pilgrim's staff as a guide and the scallop shell as a sign, they must take this long and dangerous journey, half of which is on land and half on water. Pilgrims first, then pilots.

The chapel, which has been restored and completely repainted, is of little interest, except for the ceiling vaulting, where twenty new angels carry globes on their heads and unroll scrolls. Apart from an Annunciation sculptured on the tympanum of the door, nothing remains of the symbolism, which once was there. Let us, then, enter the most curious and original room of the mansion.

A fine group, sculptured on a bracket, ornaments the room called the *Treasure Chamber*. We are told that it represents the meeting of Tristan and Isolde. I shall not contradict that and, in any case, the subject does not change the symbolic effect. This fine medieval poem is part of a cycle of Round Table romances, which are traditional hermetic legends, reviving the Greek fables. They directly concern the transmission of ancient scientific knowledge in the guise of stories, popularized by the genius of the trouvères of Picardy (pl. XL).

In the centre of the motif, a casket in the form of a cube protrudes at the foot of a bushy tree, whose foliage conceals the crowned head of King Mark. On each side appear Tristan of Lyonnesse and Isolde, the former wearing a chaperon with buriet and the latter a

[1] Mercury is the Philosophers' *holy water*. Large shells were formerly used to hold *holy water*; they are still to be found in many country churches.

crown, which she is adjusting with her right hand. Our characters are shown in the *Forest of Morois* on a carpet of long grass and flowers and they are both gazing at the mysterious hollowed-out stone, which separates them.

The myth of Tristan and Isolde offers a parallel to the myth of Theseus. Tristan fights and kills the *Mohout*, Theseus the *Minotaur*. We rediscover here the hieroglyph for the manufacture of the *Green Lion*—hence the name Tristan of *Lyonnesse*—which is taught by Basil Valentine in the form of the combat between the two champions, the *eagle* and the *dragon*. This strange encounter of chemical bodies, whose combination provides the secret solvent (and the vessel of the compound), has been the subject of many secular fables and sacred allegories. It is Cadmus, pinning the serpent to an oak tree; Apollo killing the monster Python with arrows and Jason destroying the dragon of Colchis. It is the combat between Horus and Typhon in the Osirian myth; Hercules cutting off the heads of the hydra and Perseus cutting off the Gorgon's head. St. Michael, St. George and St. Marcellus destroying the dragon are Christian counterparts of Perseus, mounted on his horse Pegasus, killing the monster which guarded Andromeda. It is also the combat between the fox and the cock, which I mentioned when describing the Paris medallions; the combat between the alchemist and the dragon (Cyliani); between the remora and the salamander (Cyrano de Bergerac); between the red serpent and the green serpent, etc.

This uncommon solvent enables the natural gold to be reincruded,[2] softened and restored to its original state in a saline, friable and very fusible form. This is the rejuvenation of the king, described by all the authors, the beginning of a new evolutionary phase, personified, in the motif we are considering, by Tristan, nephew of King Mark. In fact the uncle and the nephew are, chemically speaking, one and the same thing; of the same kind and similar in origin. The gold loses its crown—that is to say it loses its colour for a certain period—and remains deprived of it until it has reached that degree of superiority to which art or nature may carry it. It then inherits a second one, 'infinitely nobler than the first', as Limojon de St. Didier assures us.

[2] Technical hermetic term signifying being *rendered raw*, that is to revert to a state preceding maturity; being retrograded.

Thus we see the outlines of Tristan and Queen Isolde standing out clearly, while the old king remains hidden in the foliage of the central tree, which is growing out of the stone—as the tree of Jesse grows out of the chest of the patriarch. Let us also note that the queen is the wife of both the old man and of the young hero. This in accordance with hermetic tradition, which makes the king, the queen and the lover combine to form the mineral triad of the Great Work. Finally, let me describe a detail of some value to the analysis of the symbol. The tree situated behind Tristan is laden with enormous fruit—gigantic pears or figs—in such abundance that the foliage disappears in the mass of fruit. Truly it is a strange place, this Forest of *Mort-Roi* (Dead King), and how like it is to the fabulous and wonderful Garden of the Hesperides!

2

The Lallemant mansion has even more to hold our attention than Jacques Coeur's house. The mansion is a town house of modest dimensions, less ancient in style and with the rare advantage that we are able to see it in perfect state of preservation. No restoration and no mutilation have deprived it of its fine symbolical character, exemplified by abundant decoration showing delicate and minute detail. The main part of the house, built on a slope, has the lower part of the front about one storey lower than the level of the courtyard. This situation necessitates the use of a staircase, built under a semi-circular rising vault. This arrangement, which is as ingenious as it is original, affords access to the inner courtyard, from which opens the entrance to the living-rooms.

On the vaulted landing, from which the staircase begins, the guide—whom I must praise for his extreme affability—opens a small door on our right. 'Here is the kitchen,' he tells us. It is a low-ceilinged basement room, only dimly lighted by a long low window, cut from a mullion of stone, The fireplace is minute and without depth. Such is the so-called 'kitchen'. To support his statement, our guide points to a curving corbel showing a scholar grasping the handle of a pestle. Is this really the image of a broth-spoiler of the sixteenth century? I doubt it. My glance wanders from the little fireplace—where you could hardly roast a turkey, but which would be large enough to take the tower of an athenor—to the scullion, promoted cook, then round the kitchen itself, so dark and sad on this bright summer's day. . . .

The more I think about it, the less reasonable does the guide's explanation appear. This low room, separated from the dining-room by a staircase and an open courtyard, with no other fittings but a narrow, insufficient fireplace, without any iron back or pot hanger, would not logically be suitable for any culinary purpose at all. On the other hand, it seems to me to be admirably adapted to alchemical work, from which the light of the sun, the enemy of all generative processes, must be excluded. As for the scullion, I know too much about the conscientious care and the scrupulous exactitude, which the *imagers* of old used in interpreting their thought, to identify as a pestle the instrument which he is showing to the visitor. I cannot think that the artist would have failed to show also its indispensable counterpart, the mortar. Furthermore, the very form of the utensil is characteristic; what this scullion is holding is really a long-necked matrass, like those used by our chemists and which they still call *balloons* on account of their round bodies. Finally, the end of the handle of this supposed pestle is hollowed out and shaped like a whistle, which certainly proves that we are dealing with a hollow utensil, a vase or phial (pl. XLI).

This essential and very secret vessel has been given various names, chosen in such a manner as to mislead the uninitiated not only as to its real purpose but also as to its composition. The Initiates will understand me and will know what vessel I am talking about. Generally it is called the *philosophers' egg* and the *green lion*. By the term *egg*, the Wise mean their compound, prepared in its own vessel and ready to undergo the transformations which the action of the fire will produce in it. In this sense, it really is an *egg*, since its covering, or its shell, encloses the philosophers' *rebis*, composed of white and red in the same proportion as in a bird's egg. As for the second epithet, the texts have never given an interpretation of it. Batsdorff, in his *Filet d'Ariadne*, says that the philosophers gave the name *green lion* to the vessel used in the coction, but he does not give any

XLI.   LALLEMANT MANSION—BRACKET
The Vessel of the Great Work.

XLII.   LALLEMANT MANSION
The Legend of St. Christopher.

reason for this. The Cosmopolite, insisting further on the quality of the vase and its indispensability in the operation, asserts that in the Work 'there is this one *green Lion*, which closes and opens the seven indissoluble seals of the seven metallic spirits and which torments the bodies, until it has entirely perfected them, by means of the artist's long and resolute patience'. G. Aurach's manuscript[3] shows a glass matrass, half filled with *green liquid*, and adds that the whole art is based on the acquisition of this single *green Lion* and that its very name indicates its colour.

This is the *vitriol* of Basil Valentine. The third figure of the golden Fleece is almost identical with Aurach's picture. It shows a philosopher, dressed in red under a purple cloak and wearing a green cap, pointing with his right hand to a glass *matrass* containing a green liquid. Ripley is nearer to the truth when he says: 'Just a single unclean body enters our magistery; the Philosophers call it the *green Lion*. It is the medium or means of joining the tinctures between the sun and the moon.'

From these references, it appears that the vase is considered in two ways, both in its matter and in its form; on the one hand it is represented as a natural vase, on the other as an artificial one. These not very numerous or very clear descriptions, which I have just quoted, refer to the nature of the vase. A number of texts enlighten us about the form of the egg. This may equally well be round or ovoid, provided it is made of clear, transparent glass, without a flaw. Its sides must be of a certain thickness, in order to resist the internal pressures, and some authors for this reason recommend the choice of Lorraine glass.[4] Finally, the neck is long or short, according to the artist's intention or his convenience; the essential thing is that it may easily be joined to the enameller's lamp. However, these practical details are sufficiently well-known for me to be able to dispense with more detailed explanations.

For my own part, I would like above all to point out that the

[3] *Le Très précieux Don de Dieu.* Manuscript of Georges Aurach of Strasbourg, written and painted by his own hand, the year of the Salvation of redeemed Humanity. 1415.

[4] The expression Lorraine glass was formerly used to distinguish *moulded* from *blown* glass. Thanks to its moulding, the Lorraine glass could have very thick and regular sides.

ᴋ

laboratory, the place where the Adept labours, and the vase of the Work, the place where nature operates, are the two certainties which strike the initiate from the start of his visit and which make the Lallemant mansion one of the rarest and most intriguing philosophical dwellings.

Preceded by the guide, we now reach the paved courtyard. A few steps will bring us to the entrance to the *loggia* well lighted by a portico formed by three curved bays. It is a large room with a heavily beamed ceiling and it contains some monoliths, stelae and other ancient remains, which give it the appearance of a local archaeological museum. For us the interest does not lie here, but rather on the back wall, on which there is a magnificent bas-relief in painted stone. It represents St. Christopher setting down the child Jesus on the rocky bank of the legendary torrent, across which he has just brought him. In the background, a hermit with a lantern in his hand—for the scene takes place at night—is coming out of his hut and walking towards the Child-King (pl. XLII).

I have often had the good fortune to come across fine old illustrations of St. Christopher, but none has kept so close to the legend as this one. It, therefore, seems beyond doubt that the subject of this masterpiece and the text of Jacques de Voragine contain the same hermetic meaning and that, further, they have certain details not to be found elsewhere. From this fact, St. Christopher takes on the greatest significance with regard to the analogy between this giant, who carries Christ, and the gold-bearing matter Χρυσοφορος, since both play the same part in the Work. Since it is my intention to help the sincere and genuine student, I will shortly explain the esoteric meaning of this, which I kept back when speaking of the statues of St. Christopher and of the monolith standing in the Parvis Notre Dame in Paris. But, in order to make myself better understood, I shall first of all give the legendary story in the rendering by Amédée de Ponthieu[5] of the version of Jacques de Voragine. I will deliberately underline the passages and names which have a direct bearing on the work itself, its conditions and materials, so that the reader may pause, reflect and profit by them.

[5] Amédée de Ponthieu, *Légendes du Vieux Paris*. Paris, Bachelin-Deflorenne, 1867, p. 106.

'Before he was a Christian, Christopher was called *Offerus*. He was a sort of giant, dull in spirit. When he reached the age of reason, *he began to travel*, saying that he *wished to serve the greatest king on earth*. He was sent to the court of a powerful king, who was delighted to have such a strong *servant*. One day the king, hearing a singer utter the name of the devil, made the sign of the cross in terror. "Why do you do that?" Christopher asked at once. "Because I am afraid of the devil," answered the king. "If you are afraid of him, then you are not as powerful as he. So I will serve the devil." And thereupon *Offerus* departed.

'After going a long way in search of this powerful monarch, he saw a large band of horsemen coming towards him, dressed in red. Their leader, who was black, said to him: "What are you looking for?" "I am looking for the devil in order to serve him." "I am the devil, follow me." So *Offerus* enrolled himself among the servants of Satan. One day, on a long ride, the infernal band saw a cross at the roadside; the devil ordered them to turn about. "Why do you do that?" asked *Offerus*, always eager to learn. "Because I am afraid of the image of Christ." "If you are afraid of the image of Christ, then you are less powerful than he; so I will *take service with Christ*." *Offerus passed alone before the cross* and went on his way. He met *a good hermit* and asked him where he could see Christ. "Everywhere," replied the hermit. "I do not understand," said *Offerus*; but if you are telling the truth, what services can a strong and alert fellow like me do for him?" "He is served by prayer, fasting and *watching*," replied the hermit. *Offerus* made a face. "Is there no other way of pleasing him?" he asked. The recluse understood whom he was dealing with and, taking him by the hand, led him to the bank of a raging *torrent, which came down from a high mountain* and told him: "The poor people who have crossed *this water* have been drowned; stay here and carry those, who ask, across to the other side on your strong shoulders. If you do that for the love of Christ, he will recognize you as *his servant*." "I will certainly do it for the love of Christ," replied *Offerus*. So he built himself a hut on the river bank and day and night he carried across those travellers, who asked. *One night*, overcome by tiredness, he was sleeping deeply when he was awakened by a knocking at the door and heard the voice of a *child*, who called him *three times* by name. He got up, took the child on his broad shoulders and stepped into the torrent. When he reached the middle, he suddenly saw the torrent become violent. The waves swelled and hurled themselves at his sinewy legs to knock him over. He resisted as best he could, but the child's weight was like a heavy burden. Then, for fear of dropping the little traveller, he uprooted a tree in order to lean on it; but the waves went on increasing and the child became heavier and heavier. *Offerus*, afraid of drowning him, raised his head towards him and said: "Child, why do you make yourself so heavy? I feel as though I were carrying the world." The child replied: "Not only are you carrying the world, but *him who made the world*. I am Christ, your God and your master. As a reward for your good service, I baptize you in the name of my Father and in my own name and in that of the Holy Ghost; frow now on, your name will be Christopher." From that day on, Christopher went up and down the world to *teach the word* of Christ.'

This narrative shows clearly enough how faithfully the artist has observed and represented the legend down to the last details. But he has done even better than this. Under the inspiration of the hermetic scholar, who ordered the work from him,[6] he has placed the giant with his feet in the water, clothing him in some light material, knotted on the shoulder and drawn in round the waist with a broad belt. It is this belt which gives St. Christopher his real esoteric character. What I am going to say about it here is not taught elsewhere. But, apart from the fact that for many people the science taught here remains none the less obscure, I think also that a book which teaches nothing is useless and vain. For this reason, I am going to endeavour to lay bare the symbol as far as I can, in order to show to investigators of the occult the scientific fact hidden beneath the image.

Offerus' belt is marked with *crisscross lines*, like those seen on the surface of the solvent when it has been prepared according to canon law. This is the *sign*, recognized by all the Philosophers as

[6] According to certain documents preserved in the archives of the Lallemant mansion, we know that Jean Lallemant belonged to the alchemical brotherhood of the *Knights of the Round Table*.

marking exteriorly the intrinsic virtue, the perfection and the extreme purity of their mercurial substance. I have already said several times, and I will repeat again, that the whole work of the art consists in processing this mercury until it receives the above-mentioned *sign*. And this *sign* has been called by the ancient authors the *Seal of Hermes*, *Seal of the Wise (Sel des Sages*, sel, salt, being put instead of Scel, seal, which confuses the mind of seekers), the *Mark* and the *Imprint of the Almighty*, his *Signature*, also the *Star of the Magi*, *the Pole Star*, etc. This geometric pattern remains and shows up more clearly when the gold to be dissolved is put into the mercury in order to restore it to its first state, that of *young* or *rejuvenated* gold, in other words to *infant* gold. That is why mercury—that faithful servant and *Seal of the earth*—is called the *Fountain of Youth*. The Philosophers are, therefore, speaking clearly when they teach that mercury, as soon as the solution has been carried out, *bears the child*, *the Son of the Sun*, the *Little King (Kinglet)*, like a real mother, since the gold is indeed *reborn in her womb*. 'The wind—which is winged and volatile mercury—carried it in her belly', says Hermes in the Emerald Tablet. Furthermore, we find the secret version of this positive truth in the *Epiphany cake*, which it is the custom for families to eat at Epiphany, the famous feast marking the *manifestation* of the Christ *Child* to the three Magi-Kings and to the gentiles. Tradition has it that the Magi were guided to the cradle by a *star*, which was for them the *annunciatory sign*, the *Good News* of his birth. Our *cake* is signed like the matter itself and contains inside it the little child, commonly called the *bather*. It is the child Jesus, carried by Offerus, the *servant* or the *traveller*; it is the *gold in its bath*, the bather; it is the *bean*, the *sabot*, the *cradle* or the *cross* of honour and it is also the *fish* 'which swims in our philosophic water', according to the very expression of the Cosmopolite.[7] It should be noted that in the Byzantine basilicas Christ was sometimes represented, like the sirens, with a *fish*'s tail. He is shown in this way on the capital of a column in the Church of St. Brice at St. Brisson-sur-Loire (Loiret). The *fish* is the hieroglyph of the Philosophers' Stone in its first state, because the stone, like the

[7] *Cosmopolite* or *Nouvelle Lumière chymique. Traité du Sel*, p. 76. Paris, J. d'Houry, 1669.

fish, is born and lives in water. Among the paintings of the alchemical stove, made by P. H. Pfau[8] in 1702, there is one of a fisherman
with a line, drawing a fine *fish* from the water. Other allegories
recommended catching it in a *net*, which is an exact picture of the
mesh formed of intercrossed threads represented on our Epiphany
cakes.[9] Let me also mention another emblematic form, which is
rarer but no less illuminating. At a friend's house, where I was in-
vited to share this cake, I was somewhat surprised to see it decorated with an *oak* tree with spreading branches, instead of the usual
diamond pattern. The bather had been replaced by a china fish and
this *fish* was a *sole* (Lat. *sol, solis,* the sun). I will explain the hermetic meaning of the oak later, when speaking of the Golden Fleece.
Let me add that the Cosmopolite's famous fish, which he calls
Echineis, is the *oursin* (echinus, sea urchin)—the *ourson* (Little Bear),
the constellation containing the *Pole Star.* The fossilized shells of
sea urchins, which are widely found, have their surface rayed like a
star. This is the reason why Limojon de St. Didier advises investigators to direct their way 'by the sight of the *north star.*'

This mysterious fish is the *royal fish* par excellence. The one finding it in his slice of cake is given the title of *king* and is entertained
like a king. Now, the name *royal fish* used to be given to the dolphin,
the sturgeon, the salmon and the trout, because it was said that
these species were reserved for the royal table. In point of fact, this
name was only symbolical, since the *eldest son of a king,* the one
who was to wear the crown, always bore the title of *Dauphin* (dolphin) the name of a fish and, what is more, a *royal fish.* It is, moreover, a *dolphin* which the fishermen in the boat in the *Mutus Liber*
are trying to catch with *net* and hook. Similarly, dolphins are to be
seen on various decorative motifs of the Lallemant mansion: on the
middle window of the corner turret, on the capital of a pillar, as well
as on the top-piece of the little credence in the chapel. The Greek
Ikhthus of the Roman catacombs has the same origin. Indeed

[8] Kept in the museum at Winterthur (Switzerland).
[9] The popular expression *to take the cake* means to be fortunate. The
one who is fortunate enough to *find the bean in the cake* has no further
need for anything; he will never lack money. He will be doubly *king,* by
science and by fortune.

Martigny[10] reproduces a curious painting of the catacombs, showing
a fish swimming in the waves and bearing on its back a *basket* containing some loaves and a long red object, which may be a vase full
of wine. The *basket* borne by the fish is the same hieroglyph as the
cake. It also is made of intercrossed strands. Without extending
these comparisons any further, I would just like to draw the attention of the curious to the basket of Bacchus, called *cista*, which was
carried by the Cistophors in the Bacchanalian processions and 'in
which', Fr. Noel[11] tells us, 'the most mysterious thing was shut up'.

Even the very pastry of the cake obeys the laws of traditional
symbology. This pastry is *flaky* and our little *bather* is shut up in
it like a book marker. This is an interesting confirmation of the
matter represented by the Epiphany cake. Sendivogius tells us that
the prepared mercury has the aspect and form of a stony mass,
crumbly and flaky. 'If you look at it closely,' he says, 'you will notice
that it is all flaky.' Indeed, the crystalline layers, which form this
substance, lie one above the other like the *leaves of a book*; for this
reason it has been called *leafy earth, earth of leaves, book with
leaves*, etc. Thus we see the first matter of the Work expressed
symbolically as a book, sometimes open, sometimes closed, according to whether it has been worked, or merely extracted from the
mine. Sometimes, when this book is shown closed—indicating the
raw mineral substance—it is not uncommon to see it sealed with
seven bands. These are the marks of the seven successive operations, which enable it to be opened, each one breaking one of the
seven fastening seals. This is the *Great Book of Nature*, whose pages
hold the revelation of the profane sciences and of the sacred
mysteries. It is simple in style, easy to read, providing always that
one knows where to find it—which is very hard—and, above all, that
one knows how to open it—which is even more difficult.

Let us now go inside the mansion. At the end of the courtyard is
the arched door, giving access to the reception rooms. There are
some very beautiful things there and lovers of the Renaissance will
find much to satisfy their taste. Let us go through the dining room,

[10] Martigny, *Dictionnaire des Antiquités chrétiennes*, art. *Eucharistie*
2nd edition, p. 291.
[11] Fn. Noel, *Dictionnaire de la Fable*, Paris, Le Normant, 1801.

with its marvellous cloisonné ceiling and high fireplace, bearing the coats of arms of Louis XII and Anne of Britanny, and let us enter the chapel, which is a veritable jewel, lovingly carved and engraved by splendid artists. This room, which is quite short, if we except the window with its three arches bearing tracery in the gothic style, is scarcely a chapel at all. All the ornamentation is secular, all the motifs, with which it is decorated, are borrowed from hermetic science. A superb painted bas-relief, executed in the same style as the St. Christopher of the *loggia*, has as its subject the pagan myth of the Golden Fleece. The sections of the ceiling act as frames for numerous hieroglyphic figures. A pretty sixteenth-century credence presents an alchemical enigma. Here is no religious scene, no verse from the psalms, no gospel parable, nothing but the mysterious utterance of the priestly art. . . . Is it possible that this little room, so unorthodox in its adornment, but so suitable for meditation in its mystical intimacy, can have been the scene of the Philosopher's reading or prayers? Is it chapel, studio or oratory? I will leave the question unanswered.

The bas-relief of the *Golden Fleece,* which you see first of all upon entering, is a very fine landscape in stone, enhanced by colour but poorly lighted, and full of curious details, but so worn by time that these are difficult to distinguish. In the midst of an amphitheatre of mossy rocks with vertical sides, rise the rugged trunks and leafy foliage of a forest, composed mainly of oak trees. In the clearings one catches sight of various animals, which are difficult to identify—a dromedary, a bull or cow, a frog on the top of a rock, etc.—which bring life to the wild and unprepossessing scene. In the grass are growing flowers and reeds of the genus *phragmites*. On the right, a *ram*'s skin is lying on a projecting rock, guarded by a dragon, whose menacing silhouette stands out against the sky. Jason himself used to be represented at the foot of an oak tree, but this part of the composition, which was no doubt loosely connected, has become detached from the whole (pl. XLIII).

The fable of the Golden Fleece is a complete representation of the hermetic process, which results in the Philosophic stone.[12] In the language of the Adepts, the term Golden Fleece is applied to the

[12] Cf. *Alchimie,* op. cit.

XLIII.   CHAPEL OF THE LALLEMANT MANSION
The Golden Fleece.

matter prepared for the Work, as well as to the final result. This is very exact, since these substances differ only in purity, fixity and maturity. The Philosophers' Stone and the Philosophic Stone are, then, two things similar in kind and origin, but the first is raw, while the second, which is derived from it, is perfectly cooked and digested. The Greek poets tell us that 'Zeus was so pleased with the sacrifice, made in his honour by Phryxos, that he desired that all those who had this fleece should live in abundance for as long as they kept it, but that everyone should be allowed to try to win it'. One can assert without fear of contradiction that those who make use of this permission are not at all numerous. It is not that the task is impossible or even that it is extremely perilous—since anyone knowing the dragon will also know how to overcome it—but the great difficulty lies in interpreting the symbolism. How is one to reconcile satisfactorily so many diverse images, so many contradictory texts? This is, however, the only means we have of finding the right path among all those blind alleys and dead ends which are offered to us and which tempt the novice, eager to set off. Let me, therefore, never cease to urge that pupils should endeavour to solve this obscure point, which, although a material and tangible one, is the central pivot of all the symbolical combinations which we are studying.

Here truth lies veiled under two distinct images, those of the *oak* and the *ram*, which, as I have just been saying, represent *one and the same thing* under *two different aspects*. Indeed, the *oak* has always been taken by the ancient authors to indicate the common name of their initial subject as it is found in the mine. It is by means of an approximation corresponding to the *oak* that the Philosophers inform us about this matter. The phrase I use may sound ambiguous. I am sorry about that, but I cannot speak more clearly without overstepping certain limits. Only those who are initiated in the language of the gods will understand without any difficulty, since they possess the keys to unlock all doors, whether of science or of religion. But among all the would-be cabalists—so much more pretentious than knowledgeable—whether they be Jewish or Christian, how many are capable of really understanding these things? Where does one find a Tiresias, a Thales or a Melampus? It is certainly not for the would-be experts, whose illusory combinations lead to nothing concrete, positive or scientific, that I take the trouble to write. Let us leave these *doctors of the Kabbala* to their ignorance and return to our subject, which is represented hermetically by the *oak* tree.

Everyone knows that the oak often has on its leaves small, round, wrinkled excrescences, sometimes pierced by a hole, called *oak galls* (Lat. *galla*). Now, if we compare three words of the same family in Latin: *galla, Gallia, gallus*, we obtain *gall, Gaul* and the *cock*. The cock is the emblem of Gaul and the attribute of Mercury, as Jacob Tollius[13] expressly tells us. It stands on the top of the steeple in French churches and it is not without reason that France is called the eldest Daughter of the Church. We are only a step from discovering what the masters of the art have taken so much care to hide. Let us continue. The oak not only provides the *gall*, but it also gives the *kirmis* (Fr. *kermes*), which, in the Gay Science, has the same signification as Hermes, the initial consonants being interchangeable. The two terms have an identical meaning, namely *Mercury*. At any rate, while *gall* gives the name of the raw mercurial matter, *kirmis* (Arab. *girmiz that which dyes scarlet*) characterizes the prepared substance. It is important not to confuse these things if error is to be avoided when proceeding to the experiments. Remember, then, that the Philosophers' mercury, that is to say their prepared matter, must possess the virtue of dyeing and that it acquires this virtue only after the preliminary preparations.

As for the common *subject* of the Work, some call it *Magnesia lunarii*; others, who are more sincere, call it *Lead of the Wise, vegetable Saturn*. Philalethes, Basil Valentine and the Cosmopolite say *Son or Child of Saturn*. In these various names they are thinking sometimes of its magnetic property of attracting sulphur, sometimes of its fusible quality, its ease of liquefaction. For all of them it is the Holy Earth (Terra Sancta). Finally, this mineral has as its celestial hieroglyph the astronomical sign of the *Ram (Aries)*. *Gala* in Greek signifies *milk* and mercury is still called *Virgin's Milk (lac virginis)*. Therefore, brothers, if you pay attention to what I have said about the *Epiphany cake (galette des Rois)*, and if you know why the Egyptians defied the cat, you will no longer have any doubt about the

[13] *Manuductio ad Coelum chemicum.* Amstelodami, ap. J. Waesbergios, 1688.

subject which you must choose; its common name will be clearly known to you. You will then be in possession of this *Chaos of the Wise* 'in which all hidden secrets exist in potential', as Philalethes asserts, and which the skilled artist will not hesitate to actualize. Open, that is to say decompose, this matter. Try to separate the pure part of it, or its *metallic soul* as the sacred expression has it, and you will have the kirmis, the Hermes, the mercury dye which has within it the *mystic gold*, just as St. Christopher carries Jesus and the ram carries its own fleece. You will understand why the *Golden Fleece* is hung on the *oak*, like the gall and the kirmis, and you will be able to say, without violating the truth, that *the old hermetic oak acts as mother to the secret mercury*. By comparing legends and symbols, light will dawn in your mind and you will know the close affinity which unites the oak to the ram, St. Christopher to the Child-King, the Good Shepherd to the lamb, the Christian counterpart of Hermes Criophorus (the ram bearer), etc.

Leave the threshold and stand in the middle of the chapel, then raise your eyes and you will be able to admire one of the finest collections of emblems to be found anywhere.[14] This ceiling, composed of coffers arranged in three longitudinal rows, is supported towards the middle of its span by two square pillars close to the walls and bearing four grooves on their fronts.

The right hand one, as you face the only window lighting this little room, has between its spiral scrolls a human skull with two wings, which rests on a bracket. This is a graphic representation of a new procreation, deriving from putrefaction following upon the death which comes to mixtures, when they have lost their vital and volatile soul. The death of the body gives rise to a dark blue or black coloration associated with the *crow*, the hieroglyph of the *caput mortuum*[15] of the work. This is the sign and the first manifestation of dissolution, of the separation of the elements and the future

[14] Two examples of comparable treatment of initiary subjects are to be found on two wonderful ceilings. One of them, a sculpture of the sixteenth century is at Dampierre-sur-Boutonne *(Les Demeures Philosophales)*. The other example, a painted ceiling of the fifteenth century, is at Plessis-Bourré *(Deux Logis Alchimiques)*.

[15] *Translator's note: Caput mortuum*, dead head; alchemical term for residuum of a substance after distillation or sublimation.

procreation of *sulphur*, the colouring and fixed principle of metals. The two wings are put there to show that through the abandonment of the volatile and watery part, the dislocation of the parts takes place, the cohesion is broken. The body, which has mortified, falls to black ashes, which resemble coal dust. Then, through the action of the intrinsic fire developed by this dispersal, the ashes, having calcined, lose the gross impurities, which were capable of being burnt. A pure *salt* is then born, which is coloured little by little in boiling and assumes the occult power of the fire (pl. XLIV).

The capital on the left shows a decorative vase, whose mouth is flanked by two dolphins. A flower, which seems to come out of the vase, opens out into a form resembling heraldic lilies. All these symbols refer to the solvent or common mercury of the Philosophers, the opposite principle to sulphur, whose processing was emblematically indicated on the other capital.

At the base of these two supports, a large wreath of oak leaves, cut by a vertical bar decorated with the same foliage, reproduces the graphic sign which, in the spagyric art, corresponds to the common name of the subject. In this way, the wreath and the capital together form the complete symbol of the first matter, sometimes shown as an orb, which God, Jesus and some great monarchs are shown holding in their hands.

It is not my intention to analyse minutely all the images decorating the coffers of the ceiling, which is a model of its kind. The subject, which is drawn out at great length, would necessitate a special study and frequent repetition would be inevitable. I will, therefore, confine myself to giving a rapid description of it and to a summary of what is expressed by the most striking images. Among the latter, I will first mention the symbol of sulphur and its extraction from the first matter, which, as we have just seen, is graphically represented on each of the engaged pillars. It is an armillary sphere, placed on a burning fire and resembling most closely one of the pictures in the treatise on the Azoth. Here the furnace takes the place of Atlas, and this image of our practice, which is itself very instructive, needs no commentary. Not far away, an *ordinary* straw *beehive* is shown, surrounded by its bees. This is a subject frequently reproduced, especially on the alchemical stove of Winterthur. Here—and what

XLIV.   CHAPEL OF THE LALLEMANT MANSION
Capital of Pillar. Right Side.

a strange motif it is for a chapel!—is a little boy, urinating freely into his *sabot*. There, the same child, kneeling beside a pile of flat ingots, is holding an *open book*, while at his feet lies a *dead snake*. Shall I stop, or go on?—I hesitate. A detail, showing in the half-light of the mouldings, determines the meaning of this little bas-relief. The top piece of the pile bears the *star seal* of Solomon the magician king. Below is *mercury*, above the *Absolute*. The procedure is simple and complete, allowing only *one way*, requiring only *one matter*, demanding only *one operation*. 'He, who knows how to do the *Work* by the one and only mercury has found the most perfect thing.'[16] That, at least, is what the famous authors maintain. It is the union of the two triangles of fire and water, or of sulphur and mercury, combined in a single body, which produces the six-point star, the hieroglyph par excellence of the Work and of the production of the Philosophic stone. Beside this image, there is another one showing a forearm in flames, the hand snatching big *horse-chestnuts* or *sweet chestnuts*. Further on, the same hieroglyph, coming out of a rock, is holding a lighted torch. Here is the horn of Amalthea, overflowing with flowers and fruit, on which perches a *hen* or *partridge*, the bird in question not being well defined; but whether the emblem is the *black hen* or the *red partridge* makes no difference to the hermetic meaning, which it expresses. Here, now, is an overturned vase, falling from the jaws of a decorative lion, which held it suspended by a cord, which has now broken. This is an original version of the *solve et coagula* of Notre Dame of Paris. Another rather unorthodox and irreverent subject follows; this is a child trying to break a *rosary* over his knee. Further on, a large *shell*, our *scallop shell*, shows a substance fixed to it and bound with spiral scrolls. The background of the coffer bearing this image repeats fifteen times the graphic symbol, which enables the contents of the shell to be identified exactly. The same sign—substituted for the name of the matter—appears nearby. This time it is large and is in the midst of a burning furnace. In another figure we again see the child—who appears to play the part of the artist—with his feet

[16] Fulcanelli is here using the postscript to the letter which he carried about with him for many years and which is reproduced in full in the second Preface of 1957.

placed in the hollow of our famous *scallop* shell, throwing in front of
him tiny shells, which seem to have come from the big one. We also
see the *open book* consumed by fire; the radiant and flamboyant
dove surrounded by an aureole, symbol of the Spirit; the fiery *crow*,
perched on the *skull*, which it is pecking, a composite picture of
death and putrefaction; the angel *'spinning the world'* like a top,
which is a subject taken up and developed further in a little book
called *Typus Mundi*,[17] the work of some Jesuit fathers; philosophic
calcination, symbolized by a pomegranate, subjected to the action of
fire *in a vase of goldsmith's work*; above the calcinated body, the
figure 3 may be seen, followed by the letter R, which indicates to
the artist the necessity of *three repetitions* of the same procedure, on
which I have several times insisted. Finally, the following image
represents the *ludus puerorum*, mentioned in Trimosin's *Toison
d'Or* and shown in an identical manner: a boy, with his whip in the
air and a joyful expression, makes his wooden horse rear up (pl.
XLV).

I have finished my list of the principal hermetic emblems, sculptured on the ceiling of the chapel. Let me end this study by analysing
a very curious and strangely rare specimen.

Hollowed out of the wall, near the window, is a little sixteenth
century credence, which attracts attention both by the prettiness of
its decoration and by its enigma, which it is considered impossible to
solve. Never, according to our guide, has any visitor been able to
explain it. This failure stems no doubt from the fact that no one has
understood the purpose of the symbolism in the entire decoration,
or what science was concealed beneath its many hieroglyphs. The
fine bas-relief of the *Golden Fleece*, which could have served as a
guide, was not considered in its true meaning; it has remained for
everyone a mythological work, in which oriental imagination has
taken free rein. However, this credence itself bears the alchemical
imprint, the details of which I have merely tried to describe in this
work (pl. XLVI). Indeed, on the engaged pillars supporting the
architrave of this temple in miniature, we may see, directly below
the capitals, the emblems belonging to *philosophic mercury*: the
scallop shell, emblem of St. James' pilgrims or holy water container,

---

[17] *Typus Mundi.* Apud Joan. Cnobbaert, 1627.

XLV.   LALLEMANT MANSION—CHAPEL CEILING
(Detail).

XLVI.   CHAPEL OF THE LALLEMANT MANSION
Enigma of the Credence.

surmounted by the wings and trident, attributes of the sea god Neptune. This is always the same indication of the watery and volatile principle. The pediment consists of a single large decorative shell, serving as a mount for two symmetrical dolphins, joined by their tails at the top of the pediment. Three pomegranates in flames complete the ornament of this symbolic credence.

The enigma itself consists in two inscriptions: RERE, RER, which do not seem to have any meaning. Each of them is repeated *three times* on the concave back of the niche.

Thanks to this simple arrangement, I can already find a clue in the *three repetitions* of one and the same technique hidden in the mysterious expression RERE, RER. Furthermore, the *three* fiery *pomegrantes* of the pediment confirm this triple action of a single procedure, and, since they represent the *fire embodied* in this red *salt*, which is the philosophic *Sulphur*, we may easily understand that it is necessary to *repeat three times* the calcination of this body, in order to achieve the *three* philosophic *works*, àccording to the doctrine of Geber. The first operation leads primarily to the *Sulphur*, a medicine of the first order; the second operation, completely similar to the first, provides the *Elixir*, or medicine of the second order, which differs from Sulphur only in quality, not in nature; finally, the third operation, carried out like the two former ones, produces the *Philosophic Stone*, the medicine of the third order, which contains all the virtues, qualities and perfections of the Sulphur and the Elixir, multiplied in power and in extent. If anyone asks, in addition, what this triple operation consists of, whose results I have shown, and how it is carried out, I would refer the investigator to the bas-relief on the ceiling, which shows a *pomegranate* being *roasted* in a certain *vase*.

But how is one to decipher the enigma of those words devoid of meaning? In a very simple way. RE, ablative of the Latin *res*, means the *thing*, regarded in its material aspect. Since the word RERE is the union of RE, *a thing*, and RE, *another thing*, I translate it as *two things in one* or *a double thing*. RERE is thus the equivalent of RE BIS (a thing twice). If you open a hermetic dictionary or turn over the pages of any alchemical work, you will find that the word REBIS, frequently used by the Philosophers, stands for their *com-*

post, or compound ready to undergo the successive metamorphoses under the influence of fire. I will continue. RE, a dry matter, *philosophic gold*; RE, a humid matter, *philosophic mercury*; RERE or REBIS, a double matter, at once both dry and humid, the amalgam of philosophic gold and mercury, a combination which has received a *double* occult *property*, exactly equilibrated, from nature and from art.

I would like to be equally clear about the explanation of the second term RER, but I am not allowed to tear down the veil of mystery concealing it. Nevertheless, in order to satisfy as far as possible the legitimate curiosity of the children of the art, I will say that these three letters contain a vitally important secret, referring to the *vase of the work*. RER is used to cook, to unite radically and indissolubly, to activate the transformations of the compost RERE. How am I to give sufficient hints, without breaking my vow? Do not trust what Basil Valentine says in his *Douze Clefs* and be careful not to take his words literally, when he alleges that 'he, who has the matter, will easily find a pot to cook it in.' I maintain, on the contrary—and you may have faith in my sincerity—that it will be impossible to obtain the slightest success in the Work, if you do not know perfectly what this *Philosophers' Vase* is, nor from what material it must be made. Pontanus confesses that before knowing this secret vessel he had begun the same work again more than two hundred times without success, although he was working on right and suitable matters and using the proper method. The artist must *make* his vessel *himself*; that is a maxim of the art. Do not, therefore, undertake anything until you have received all the light on this eggshell, which the masters of the Middle Ages called the *secretum secretorum* (secret of secrets).

What, then, is this RER?—We have seen that RE means *a thing, a matter*; R, which is *half* RE, will mean *a half thing* or *a half matter*. RER, then, is the equivalent of a matter increased by half of another or of itself. Note that it is not here a question of proportions, but of a chemical combination independent of relative quantities. In order to make myself better understood, let me give an example. Let us suppose that the matter represented by RE is *realgar*, or natural sulphur of arsenic. R, half RE, could then be the *sulphur* of the realgar or its *arsenic*, which are similar or different according to whether you consider the sulphur and the arsenic separately or combined in the realgar. In this way the RER will be obtained by *augmenting* the realgar with sulphur, which is considered as forming half the realgar, or with arsenic, which is seen as the other half in the same red sulphide.

Here is some more advice: seek first the RER, that is to say the *vessel*. After that the RERE will easily be recognizable to you. The Sibyll, when asked what a Philosopher was, replied: 'It is a man, who knows how to make glass.' Apply yourself to making it according to our art, without paying too much attention to the processes of glass-making. The potter's craft would be more instructive for you. Look at Picolpassi's plates,[18] you will find one showing a *dove with its claws attached to a stone*. Must you not, according to the excellent advice of Tollius, seek and find the magistery in something *volatile*? But if you possess no vase to hold it, how will you prevent it from evaporating, from being dissipated without leaving the least trace? Therefore, make your vase, then your compound; seal it with care, in such a way that no spirit may escape; heat the whole according to the art until it is calcined. Return the pure part of the powder obtained to your compound, which you will seal up in the same vase. Repeat for the third time and do not give me any thanks. Your thanksgiving must be directed only to the Creator. As for me, I am nothing but a beacon on the great highway of the esoteric Tradition. I ask for neither remembrance nor gratitude, but only that you should take the same trouble for others as I have taken for you.

Our tour is over. Once again we stand in pensive and silent wonder, pondering on these marvellous and surprising exemplars, whose author has so long remained unknown to us. Is there somewhere a book written in his hand? Nothing seems to indicate it. No doubt, following the example of the great Adepts of the Middle Ages, he preferred to entrust to stone, rather than to vellum, the undeniable evidence of an immense science, of which he possessed all the secrets. It is, therefore, just and equitable that his memory

[18] Claudius Popelin, *Les Trois Livres de l'Art du Potier*, by the Knight Cyprian Piccolpassi. Paris, Librairie Internationale, 1861.

L

should be revived among us, that his name should at last emerge from obscurity and shine like a star of the first magnitude in the hermetic firmament.

Jean Lallemant, alchemist and Knight of the Round Table, deserves to take his place round the Holy Grail, to have communion there with Geber (Magister Magistrorum) and with Roger Bacon (Doctor admirabilis). He equals the mighty Basil Valentine, the charitable Flamel, in the range of his knowledge, but excels them in expressing two eminently scientific and philosophical qualities, which he carried to the highest degree of perfection, namely modesty and sincerity.

The Cyclic Cross
of Hendaye

Hendaye, a small frontier town in the Basque country, has its little houses huddled at the foot of the first spurs of the Pyrenees. It is framed by the green ocean, the broad, swift and shining Bidassoa and the grassy hills. One's first impression, on seeing this rough and rugged landscape, is a rather painful and almost hostile one. On the horizon, over the sea, the natural austerity of the wild scene is scarcely relieved by the headland of Fuenterrabia, showing ochre in the crude light, thrusting into the dark greyish-green mirror-calm waters of the gulf. Apart from the Spanish character of its houses, the type of dialect of the inhabitants, and the very special attraction of a new beach, bristling with proud villas,

Hendaye has nothing to hold the attention of the tourist, the archaeologist or the artist.

Leaving the station, a country road, skirting the railway line, leads to the parish church, situated in the middle of the village. This church, with its bare walls and its massive, squat rectangular tower, stands in a square a few steps above ground level and bordered by leafy trees. It is an ordinary, dull building, which has been renovated and is of no particular interest. However, near the south transept there is a humble stone cross, as simple as it is strange, hiding amidst the greenery of the square. It was formerly in the parish cemetery and it was only in 1842 that it was brought to its present site near the church. At least, that is what was told me by an old Basque man, who had for many years acted as sexton. As for the origin of this cross, it is unknown and I was not able to obtain any information at all about the date of its erection. However, judging by the shape of the base and the column, I would not think that it could be before the end of the seventeenth or beginning of the eighteenth century. Whatever its age, the Hendaye cross shows by the decoration of its pedestal that it is the strangest monument of primitive millenarism, the rarest symbolical translation of chiliasm,[1] which I have ever met. It is known that this doctrine, first accepted and then refuted by Origen, St. Denis of Alexandria and St. Jerome although it had not been condemned by the Church, was part of the esoteric tradition of the ancient hermetic philosophy.

The naivety of the bas-reliefs and their unskilful execution lead one to suppose that these stone emblems were not the work of a professional sculptor; but, aesthetic considerations apart, we must recognize that the unknown workman, who made these images, possessed real and profound knowledge of the universe.

On the transverse arm of the cross—a Greek cross—is found the following inscription, consisting of two strange parallel lines of raised letters, forming words almost running into each other, in the same order as I give here:

OCRUXAVES

PESUNICA

[1] *Translator's note:* millenarism, chiliasm, doctrine of belief in the millenium.

Certainly it is easy to recognize the well-known phrase: *O crux ave spes unica* (Hail o cross, the only hope). However, if we were to translate it like a schoolboy, we should not know the purpose either of the base or of the cross and we might be surprised by such an invocation. In reality, we should carry carelessness and ignorance to the pitch of disregarding the elementary rules of grammar. The masculine word *pes* in the nominative requires the adjective *unicus*, agreeing in gender, and not the feminine form *unica*. It would, therefore, appear that the corruption of the word *spes*, hope, into *pes*, foot, by dropping the initial consonant, must be the unintentional result of a complete lack of knowledge on the part of our stone-cutter. But does inexperience really justify such uncouthness? I cannot think so. Indeed, a comparison of the other motifs, carried out by the same hand and in the same manner, shows evident care to reproduce the normal positioning, a care shown both in the placing and in the balance of the motifs. Why should the inscription have been treated less scrupulously? A careful examination of the latter shows that the letters are clear, if not elegant, and do not overlap (pl. XLVII). No doubt our workman traced them first in chalk or charcoal, and this rough draft must rule out any idea that a mistake occurred during the actual cutting of the letters. However, since this *apparent* mistake exists, it follows that it must really have been intended. The only reason that I can think of is that it is a *sign put in on purpose*, concealed under the appearance of an inexplicable blunder, and intended to arouse the curiosity of the observer. I will, therefore, state that, in my opinion, it was with knowledge and intent that the author arranged the inscription of his puzzling work in this way.

I had already been enlightened by studying the pedestal and knew in what way and by means of what key the Christian inscription of the monument should be read; but I was anxious to show investigators what help may be obtained in solving hidden matters from plain common sense, logic and reasoning.

The letter S, which takes on the curving shape of a snake, corresponds to the Greek *khi* (X) and takes over its esoteric meaning. It is the helicoidal track of the sun, having arrived at the zenith of its curve across space, at the time of the cyclic catastrophe.

It is a theoretical image of the *Beast of the Apocalypse*, of the dragon, which, on the days of Judgment, spews out fire and brimstone on macrocosmic creation. Thanks to the symbolic value of the letter S, displaced on purpose, we understand that the inscription must be translated in secret language, that is to say in the *language of the gods* or the *language of the birds*, and that the meaning must be found with the help of the rules of *Diplomacy*. Several authors, and particularly Grasset d'Orcet in his analysis of the *Songe de Polyphile* published by the *Revue Britannique*, have given these sufficiently clearly to make it unnecessary for me to repeat them. We shall, then, read in *French*, the language of the diplomats, the Latin just as it is written. Then, by making use of the permutation of vowels, we shall be able to read off the new words, forming another sentence, and re-establish the spelling, the word order and the literary sense. In this way we obtain the following strange announcement: *Il est écrit que la vie se réfugie en un seul espace* (It is written that life takes refuge in a single space)[2] and we learn that a country exists, where death cannot reach man at the terrible time of the double cataclysm. As for the geographical location of this promised land, from which the élite will take part in the return of the golden age, it is up to us to find it. For the élite, the children of Elias, will be saved according to the word of Scripture, because their profound faith, their untiring perseverence in effort, will have earned for them the right to be promoted to the rank of disciples of the Christ-Light. They will bear his sign and will receive from him the mission of renewing for regenerated humanity the chain of tradition of the humanity which has disappeared.

The front of the cross, the part which received the three terrible nails fixing the agonized body of the Redeemer to the accursed wood, is indicated by the inscription INRI, carved on its transverse arm. It corresponds to the schematic image of the cycle, shown on the base (pl. XLVIII). Thus we have two symbolic crosses, both instruments of the same torture. Above is the divine cross, exemplifying the chosen means of expiation; below is the global

---

[2] Latin *spatium*, with the meaning of *place*, *situation*, given to it by Tacitus. It corresponds to the Greek Χωρίον, root Χωρα, *country*, *territory*.

XLVII.   HENDAYE (Basses-Pyrénées)
Cyclic Cross.

XLVIII.   CYCLIC CROSS OF HENDAYE
The four Sides of the Pedestal.

cross, fixing the pole of the *northern hemisphere* and locating in time the fatal period of this expiation. God the Father holds in his hand this globe, surmounted by the *fiery sign*. The four great ages—historical representations of the four ages of the world—have their sovereigns shown holding this same attribute. They are Alexander, Augustus, Charlemagne and Louis XIV.[3] It is this which explains the inscription INRI, exoterically translated as *Iesus Nazarenus Rex Iudeorum* (Jesus of Nazareth, King of the Jews), but which gives to the cross its secret meaning: *Igne Natura Renovatur Integra* (By fire nature is renewed whole). For it is by fire and in fire that our hemisphere will soon be tried. And just as, by means of fire, gold is separated from impure metals, so, Scripture says, the good will be separated from the wicked on the great Day of Judgment.

On each of the four sides of the pedestal, a different symbol is to be seen. One has the image of the sun, another of the moon; the third shows a great star and the last a geometric figure, which, as I have just said, is none other than the diagram used by the initiates to indicate the solar cycle. It is a simple circle, divided into four sectors by two diameters cutting each other at right angles. The sectors each bear an A, which shows that they stand for the four ages of the world. This is a complete hieroglyph of the universe, composed of the conventional signs for heaven and earth, the spiritual and the temporal, the macrocosm and the microcosm, in which major emblems of the redemption (cross) and the world (circle) are found in association.

In medieval times, these four phases of the great cyclic period, whose continuous rotation was expressed in antiquity by means of a circle divided by two perpendicular diameters, were generally represented by the four evangelists or by their symbolic letter, which was the Greek *alpha*, or, more often still, by the four evangelical beasts surrounding Christ, the living human representation of the cross. This is the traditional formula, which one meets frequently on the tympana of Roman porches. Jesus is shown there seated, his

[3] The first three are emperors, the fourth is only a king, the Sun King, thus indicating the decline of the star and its last radiation. This is dusk, the forerunner of the long cyclic night, full of horror and terror, 'the abomination of desolation'.

left hand resting on a book, his right raised in the gesture of bene-diction, and separated from the four beasts, which attend him, by an ellipse, called the *mystic almond*. These groups, which are generally isolated from other scenes by a garland of clouds, always have their figures placed in the same order, as may be seen in the cathedrals of Chartres (royal portal) and Le Mans (west porch), in the Church of the Templars at Luz (Hautes Pyrénées) and the Church of Civray (Vienne), on the porch of St. Trophime at Arles, etc. (pl. XLIX).

'And before the throne,' writes St. John, 'there was a sea of glass, like unto crystal: and in the midst of the throne, and round about the throne, were four beasts full of eyes before and behind. And the first beast was like a lion, and the second beast like a calf, and the third beast had a face as a man, and the fourth beast was like a flying eagle.'[4]

This agrees with Ezekiel's version: 'And I looked, and behold . . . a great cloud, and a fire infolding itself and a brightness was about it, and out of the midst thereof as the colour of amber, out of the midst of the fire. Also out of the midst thereof came the likeness of four living creatures. . . . As for the likeness of their faces, they four had the face of a man, and the face of a lion on the right side; and they four had the face of an ox on the left side; they four also had the face of an eagle.'[5]

In Hindu mythology, the four equal sectors of the circle, formed by the cross, were the basis of a rather strange mystical conception. The entire cycle of human evolution is figured there in the form of a cow, symbolizing Virtue, each of whose four feet rests on one of the sectors representing the four ages of the world. In the first age, corresponding to the Greek age of gold and called the *Creda Yuga* or *age of innocence*, Virtue is firmly established on earth: the cow stands squarely on four legs. In the *Treda Yuga* or second age, corresponding to the age of silver, it is weakened and stands only on three legs. During the *Touvabara Yuga*, or third age, which is the age of bronze, it is reduced to two legs. Finally, in the age of iron, our own age, the cyclic cow or human virtue reaches the

---

[4] Revelation, ch. 1v, v. 6 and 7.
[5] *Ezekiel*, ch. I, v. 4, 5, 10 and 11.

utmost degree of feebleness and senility: it is scarcely able to stand, balancing on only one leg. It is the fourth and last age, the *Kali Yuga*, the age of misery, misfortune and decrepitude.

The *age of iron* has no other seal than that of *Death*. Its hieroglyph is the skeleton, bearing the attributes of Saturn: the empty hourglass, symbol of time run out, and the scythe, reproduced in the figure seven, which is the number of transformation, of destruction, of annihilation. The Gospel of this fatal age is the one written under the inspiration of St. Matthew. *Matthaeus*, Greek Ματθαὶος, comes from Μάθημα, Μάθηματος, which means science. This word has given Μάθησις, μάθησεωʂ, study, knowledge, from μανθάνειν, to learn. It is the Gospel according to Science, the last of all but for us the first, because it teaches us that, save for a small number of the élite, we must all perish. For this reason the angel was made the attribute of St. Matthew, because science, which alone is capable of penetrating the mystery of things, of beings and their destiny, can give man wings to raise him to knowledge of the highest truths and finally to God.

XLIX.   ARLES—CHURCH OF ST. TROPHIME
Tympanum of the Porch (XIIth Century).

Conclusion

Scire, Potere, Audere, Tacere
ZOROASTER

Nature does not open the door of the sanctuary indiscriminately to everyone.

In these pages, the uninitiated will perhaps discover some proof of a genuine and positive science. I do not, however, flatter myself that I shall convert them, for I know full well the obstinacy of prejudice and the great strength of preconceived opinions. The disciple will derive greater benefit from this book, provided always that he does not despise the works of the old Philosophers and that he studies with care and penetration the classical text, until he has acquired sufficient perception to understand the obscure points of the practice.

No one may aspire to possess the great secret, if he does not direct his life in accordance with the researches he has undertaken.

It is not enough to be studious, active and persevering, if one has no firm principles, no solid basis, if immoderate enthusiasm blinds one to reason, if pride overrules judgment, if greed expands before the prospect of a golden future.

The mysterious science requires great precision, accuracy and perspicacity in observing the facts, a healthy, logical and reflective mind, a lively but not over-excitable imagination, a warm and pure heart. It also demands the greatest simplicity and complete indifference with regard to theories, systems and hypotheses, which are generally accepted without question on the testimony of books or the reputation of their authors. It requires its candidates to learn to think more with their own brains and less with those of others. Finally, it insists that they should check the truth of its principles, the knowledge of its doctrine and the practice of its operations from nature, the mother of us all.

By constant exercise of the faculties of observation and reasoning and by meditation, the novice will climb the steps leading to

KNOWLEDGE

A simple imitation of natural processes, skill combined with ingenuity, the insight born of long experience will secure for him the

POWER

Having obtained that, he will still have need of patience, constancy and unshakeable will. Brave and resolute, he will be enabled by the certainty and confidence born of a strong faith to

DARE

Finally, when success has crowned so many years of labour,

when his desires have been accomplished, the Wise Man, despising the vanities of the world, will draw near to the humble, the disinherited, to all those who work, suffer, struggle and weep here below. As an anonymous and dumb disciple of eternal Nature, an apostle of eternal Charity, he will remain faithful to his vow of silence.

In Science, in Goodness, the Adept must evermore

KEEP SILENT

Index

INDEX

Abbon, 77
Abraham the Jew (Eleazor), 75, 81, 92
Absolom-Absolute, 49, 157
Aegidius de Vadis, 132
Agent or secret fire, 80
Agricola, 71
Agriculture, celestial, 91
Alchemist of Notre-Dame, 72
Alkahest, 94, 99, 102
Allot (Abbé), 60
Amiens cathedral, 123
Amyraut (M), 47
Ankh or crux ansata, 46
Anonymity, 8
Apollo and Python, 142
Apollonius of Tyana, 44
Argonauts, 42, 103
Argotiers, 42
Ariadne or the spider, 48, 90
Aries or the ram, 84, 92, 154
Aristotle, 64, 97, 114
Arnold of Villanova, 94
Art of light, 43
Artephius, 83, 105, 131
Assation, 49
Athenor, 78, 89, 127
Aurach (Georges), 145

Babe lying in a manger, 54
Bacon (Roger), 162
Balaam, 55
Basil Valentine, 9, 13, 15, 74, 94, 97, 100, 110, 128, 130, 142, 145, 154, 160
Basket of Bacchus, 151
Basket of the catacombs, 151
Bath of the stars, 107
Batsdorff, 81, 144
Bernard Trévisan, 73, 80, 92, 101, 108
Berthelot (Marcelin), 48
Bigarne (Ch.), 57
Bird of Hermes, 90
Black cloud, 80
Black hen, 85
Black pitch, 80

Black stone fallen from heaven, 61
Blessed ones or initiates, 85
Boeswillwald (E), 41
Bonetty (A), 55
Book with leaves, 71, 151
Briareus, 100
Bull, 95

Cabala, phonetic, 17
Cabot, 39
Cadmus and the serpent, 74, 93, 96, 181
Calcination, 82
Callimachus, 90
Cambriel (L. P. François), 115, 116
Candles, green, 60
Castaigne (R. P. de), 98
Cat, 154
Cavern of the Rock, 52
Celestial dew, 107, 133
Centaur, 17
Chabot, 39
Chalcidius, 54
Champagne (Julien), 7, 17
Chaos, metallic, chaos of the Wise, 74, 131, 155
Chaos, primitive, 14, 74, 85
Charity, 11
Chaudet, 119
Chevalier Inconnu (le), 79
Child, divine, 13
Child of Saturn, 154
Child, the beginning and the end, 53
Children of the sun, 43
Child's play (ludus puerorum), 125, 158
Christopher (cabala), 64
Cimiez, 13
Cimmerian darkness, 85
Claves (Gaston de), 81
Coat of arms, symbolic, 119
Cock and fox, 95, 101, 128, 142
Cock crow, 129
Cohobation, 96, 103
Colfs (J. F.), 36
Colour, black, 50, 79, 89
Colour, red, 50, 89

Colour, white, 50, 89
Colours, elemental, 86
Colours symbolical of the Great Work, 50, 84, 89
Conception, 13
Condensation of the universal spirit, 107, 134
Conjunction, 90, 95, 101, 106
Constantine, 45
Cormont (Renault and Thomas de), 124
Corneille (Thomas), 107
Corner stone, 47
Correspondance of metallic planets, 97
Cosmic magic, 14
Cosmopolite (the), 46, 84, 92, 97, 102, 104, 145, 149, 154
Court language, 44
Court of Miracles, 42
Cross, 45
Cross, starred, 52
Crow, black, 78, 88, 155, 158
Crow of Notre Dame, 106
Crow's head, 79, 81
Crucible, 45, 111
Crux ansata, 46
Crypts of cathedrals, 56
Cum luce salutem, 13
Cyliani, 9, 13, 111, 142
Cyrano de Bergerac, 17, 102, 142

David (Louis), 86
Dauphin, 150
Demetrius, 100
'Demeures Philosophales', 10, 17
Despartes (Jacques), 39
'Deux Logis Alchimiques', 17, 155
Devil of Notre-Dame, 46
Devilry of Chaumont, 39
Dew-grease, 134
Dew of May, 94, 108
Diodorus of Tarsus, 54
Dissolution, radical, 96
Dive-Bouteille, 44
Divine light, 10
Dog of Corascene, 105
Door of the temple, 13

Dove fixed to the stone, 161
Doves of Diana, 105
'Douze Clefs de la Philosophie', 9, 13, 93, 95, 160
Dragon, Babylonian, 114
Dragon, fiery, 14
Du Cange, 45
Dujols (Pierre), 72, 85
Durand (Georges), 124, 126, 128
Durandal, 65

Eagle, to make the eagle fly, 90
Eagle and lion, 89, 90, 91, 101
Eagle with a cross, 53
Eagles or sublimations, 90
Eagles, seven or nine, 90
Earth-butter, 134
Earth, holy, 154
Earth, philosophic, 14
Earth, virgin, 58
Echeneis, 150
Eclipse of the sun, 80
Elixation, 125
Emerald of the philosophers, 94
Epistle of the Immaculate Conception, 70
Epiphany cake, 150
Essarts (Antoine des), 64
Eternal truth, 9
Etteila (Alliette), 71, 89
Evans (Dr.), 49
Exaltation and transfusion, 98
Extraction of sulphur, 95

Faithful servant, 149
Fasting man of Notre-Dame, 63
Feast of the Donkey, 38
Feast of Fools, 37
Fire of the wheel, 50, 100, 124, 126
Fire, secret, 14, 50, 80, 82, 83, 94
Fire, subterranean, 63
Fish's eyes, 80
Fish, symbolic, 149
Flag, French, 86
Flagellation of the Alleluia, 39
Flamboyant Gothic, 50
Flamel (Nicholas), 74, 75, 92, 107, 118, 132, 141

Flammarion (Camille), 60
Flower, heavenly, 134
Fortress, alchemical, 130
Foul smell, 81, 89
Fountain of Youth, 77, 149
Fountain, mysterious, 73, 75, 76
Fraternities, secret, 139
Fulcanelli, 6, 7, 9, 12, 13
Fundament, celestial, 134

Gall, 154
Gay science, gay knowledge, 18, 44
Geber, 109, 129, 159
Geffroy Dechaume, 41
Generation, 135
Gideon's fleece, 71
Gift of God, 8, 10
Glass, 11
Glass of Lorraine, 145
Glass matrass, 145
Gobineau de Montluisant (Esprit), 114
Gohorny (Jean), 119
Gold, mystic, 155
Gold in its bath, 149
Golden fleece, 12, 152, 155, 158
Good tidings, good news, 54, 149
Goose, 90
Gothic art, 41
Grasset d'Orcet, 168
Gravier (Antoine), 59
Gregory of Tours, 77
Grey, dealer in, 63
Griffin, 89, 93
Grillot de Givry, 109
Grosson, 61
Guillaume de Paris, 63, 103, 106, 123

Hames (Guillaume de), 60
Haymon, 132
Helvetius (Johann Friedrich), 15, 16, 111
Henckel (J. F.), 111
Hendaye, cross of, 166
Herald of the Mysteries of Ceres, 61
Herb of Saturn, 94
Hermes Trismegisthus, 81, 149

Herodotus, 61
Hierophant, 61
Hiram (masonic), 48
Holmat, 75
Holy water containers, 141, 158
Horus and Typhon, 142
House of Gold, 71
Huginus à Barma, 53, 97, 109

Illumination, 8
Infanterie dijonnaise, 39
Initiator, true, 10
INRI, 168
Isis, prototype of black virgins, 57, 61, 136

Jacques Coeur, 140
Jacques Coeur's house, 139
John's blackbird, 80
Jourdain and Duval, 124, 126, 128
Julius Africanus, 53

Kabbala, 17, 154
Kermis, 154
Khunrath (Heinrich), 130
Kinglet, 149

Laborde (de), 111
Labour of Hercules, 102
Labourer, 91
Labyrinth of Amiens, 47
Labyrinth of the cathedrals, 48
Labyrinth of Chartres, 47
Labyrinth of Cnossos, 49
Ladder of the philosophers, 70
Lagneau (David), 119
Lallemant (Jean), 148, 162
Lallemant mansion, 143
Lamb, mystic, 45, 105
Language of colours, 84
Language of the gods, or of the birds, 18, 44, 168
Lassus (J. B. A.), 36, 41
Latten, 46, 103
Lead, 15
Leafy earth, 151
Leboeuf (Abbé), 63
Le Breton, 79, 133
Lenglet-Dufresnoy (Abbé), 90, 110

Lepers, curing of, 86
Leprosy, mineral, 81
Libethra of Magnesia, 74
Liébaut (Jean), 128
Limojon de St. Didier, 82, 83, 142, 150
Linthaut (Henri de), 111
Lion, 93
Lion, red, 94, 96, 101
Lion, green, 94, 96, 101, 142, 144
Little world, 14
Life hidden in matter, 46
Lodestone, philosophic or magnet, 15, 49, 92, 133
Lost word, verbum dimissum, 108, 131
Lucifer, 47
Lully (Raymond), 80, 98, 109

Mad mother, 39
Magi, wise men, 14, 52
Magistery, 12
Magnesia of the Wise, 48, 74, 80, 134
Mangin de Richebourg (J.), 73
Mark, divine, 13
Martigny, 151
Massacre of the ·Innocents, 76, 107, 120
Master stone, 63
Matrices, 69
Matter of the Wise, 133
Medicine of the three orders, 82, 159
Melampus, 44
Mercury, animated, 90, 102
Mercury, common of the philosophers, 12, 97, 156
Mercury, philosophic, 81, 98, 160
Messire Le Gris (Mr. Grey), 63
Metallic natures, 113, 132
Metallic seed, 82
Milk and blood, 75
Mineral theophany, 17
Minister of the altar, 61
Mirror of the art, 12, 96
Mirror of Mars, 15
Modhallam, 75

Molten lead, 80
Moon-spit, 134
Moras de Respour, 96
Morien, 80, 133
Mortification of Mercury, 81
Mother of the gods, 58, 61
Mother tongue, 17
Mount of Victory, 52
Mullachius, 54
Multiplications of the stone, 116
Mysterious palace, 100, 130

Naxagoras, 16
Noël (Fr.), 74, 151
Noël du Fail, 40
Nostoc, 134
Notre-Dame-de-Confession, 59
Notre-Dame-du-Pilier, 58
Notre-Dame-sous-Terre, 58
Nuysement (de), 50

Oak, hollow, 74, 76, 93, 128
Oak and ram, 153, 155
Oak on the Epiphany cake, 150
Obedience, 9
Obscurity, complete, 135
Orientation of churches, 49
Osiris, black, 86

Paracelsus, 86, 109
Paris cathedral, 69
Père Abraham, 83
Pernety (Dom A. J.), 97, 109, 125
Pfau (P. H.), 150
Pheasant, 90
Phidias, 61
Philalethes (Eyreneus), 14, 15, 90, 98, 100, 105, 110, 126, 130, 154
Philosophers' lead, 85, 154
Philosophic egg, 61, 89, 144
Phoebigenus, 63
Phoenix, 129
Phrygian cap, 72
Phtah the regenerator, 86
Piccolopassi (Cyprian), 161
Pierre de Corbeil, 38
Pierre du Coignet, 46
Pierre de Montereau, 120

Pilgrim or mercury, 141, 149
Planetary metals, 104
Plessis-Bourré, 17
Plutarch, 100
Poeris, 101
Poisson (Albert), 118, 119, 126
Pontanus, 83, 160
Ponthieu (Amadée de), 63, 146
Popelin (Claudius), 161
Portal (Frédéric), 85
Processes of the Stone, 87
Procession of the Fox, 38
Procession of the Shrovetide Carnival, 39
Puss-in-Boots, 39
Putrefaction of the Work, 78, 81

Quintessence, 115

Ram, symbolic, 84, 102, 152
Rebis, hermetic, 79, 100, 144, 159
Reduction, metallurgic, 16
Régime of Saturn, 110
Reincrudation, 100, 142
Repetition, 158
Renewal, 85
Renunciation, 9
Restoration of cathedrals, 41
Rex ab igne veniet, 114
Ripley (George), 100, 145
Robert de Luzarches, 124
Rock, 74
Rollin (Nicholas), 136
Root or principle, 72
Rose-Cross, 107
Rose, mystic, 71
Rose windows, 51
Roses, black, 85
Roses, white and red, 76
Royalty, true, 11
Roze (Abbé), 126
Ruskin (John), 124, 127

Sabot, 38, 157
Sacred wells in churches, 77
St. Amadour, 59
St. Augustine, 45
St. Christopher, 64, 146, 148, 155

St. Christopher, legend of, 147
St. Chrysostom, 13
St. Ignatius, 53
St. James, 158
St. John, 170
St. Luke, 54
St. Marcellus, 111, 117, 142
St. Matthew, 55, 171
St. Michael, 142
St. Paul, 131
St. Peter, 129
St. Thomas Aquinas, 119
Salamander, 82, 142
Salamander and remora, 102, 142
Salmon (Guillaume), 118
Salt of the red lion, 96
Salt of the philosophers, 114, 149
Saturn, black, 85
Saturn, green god, 101
Saturn of the Wise, 15, 115
Schadius (Elias), 58
Sea, dark and gloomy, 75
Seal of Hermes, 149
Seal, magic, 51
Seal, royal, 15
Seat of wisdom, 71
Secret, 13, 131, 176
Self, former, 9
Sendivogius (see Cosmopolite), 151
Separation, 14
Serpents, red and green, 142
Servus fugitivus, 99
Seth (Book of), 52
Shadows, 81
Shell of Compostella, 141, 157
Sign, hermetic, 54
Signature of the Epiphany cake, 149
Signature of the Work, 136
Sky, chemical, 13
Sky, terrestial, 14
Snake of Hermes, 81
Solomon, 14, 48, 51
Solomon's seal, 51, 157
Solve et coagula, 105, 157
Son of Saturn, 154
Son of the sun, 43, 136, 149
Soul, metallic, 107, 155
Spirit of the green lion, 96

Spirits of salt, 15
Star and conception, 56
Star, hermetic, 14
Star of Jacob, 56
Star of the Magi, 5
Star of the morning, 13, 47
Star, nocturnal, 13
Star of the sea, 49
Star, terrestial, 54
Stars, two, 13
Steel, magic, 15
Steel, philosophic, 92
Stone which is not stone, 132
Stuart de Chevalier (Sabine), 99
Subject of the Wise, 71, 73, 100
Sublimations, 90
Sulphur, embodied, 107
Sulphur, philosophic, 116
Sulphur, principle, 46
Sun, moon and stars, 53, 130
Swan of Hermes, 90
Swift (Jonathan), 18

Temperature of fire, 125
Thales of Miletus, 44, 153
Thread of Ariadne, 48, 144
Ticinensis, 71
Tinctorial mass, 11
Tiresias, 44, 153
Tollius (Jacobus), 14, 88, 154
Torchbearer, 61
Toussaint, 41
Tower of Babel, 44
Tradition, 9, 161
Traveller, synonym of Mercury, 141
Treasure of treasures, 10
Tree of life, 97
Tree, solar, 102
Trémelles, 134
Trismosin (Solomon), 76, 110, 158
Tristan and Isolde, 142
Triumphal chariot of Bacchus, 37

Universal solvent, 83, 92, 99
Universal spirit, 14, 94, 107

Valois (Nicholas), 70, 132
Varro, 51

Vase of the art and of nature, 145, 160
Vase of the spirit, 71
Vegetable stone, 94
Verbum dimissum, 6, 108, 131
Vessel of the Great Work, 92, 93, 161
Victor Hugo, 40, 106, 120
Vigenère (Blaise de), 16
Villain (Abbé), 118
Villon (François), 42
Vincens (Charles), 61
Vinceslas Lavinius of Moravia, 14
Vinegar, mercurial, 93
Viollet-le-Duc, 41
Virgin, celestial, 13
Virgin-mother, 70, 108
Virgin, mystical, 13
Virgins, black, 57
Virgin's milk, 74, 154
Virtue, urano-diurnal, 54
Vitriol, 97, 145
Vitriol, green of the Wise, 94
Vitriol, vegetable, 134
'Vitulus Aureus', 15
Voragine (Jacques de), 64, 146
Voyous, voyants, 43
Vulcan, 15

Water, burning or fiery, 82
Water, dry which does not wet the hands, 74, 84, 129
Water of life, 103
Water, pontic, 77, 102
Water, primitive, 83
Ways, moist and dry, 109, 110
West, 81
Witkowski (G. J.), 38, 56, 58, 60, 75
Wheel, 50
White stone, 140
Work by the one and only mercury, 82, 157

Zachaire (Denys), 40, 62
Zacchaeus, 59
Zadith (Senior), 75, 110
Zodiac, 106
Zoroaster, 175